Diversity of Migrant Entrepreneurship in Varieties of European Capitalism

Sanja Tepavcevic

Diversity of Migrant Entrepreneurship in Varieties of European Capitalism

Post-Soviet Entrepreneurship in Austria, Spain and Hungary

palgrave
macmillan

Sanja Tepavcevic
Institute of Advanced Studies Koszeg
University of Pannonia
Kőszeg, Hungary

ISBN 978-3-031-31096-6 ISBN 978-3-031-31097-3 (eBook)
https://doi.org/10.1007/978-3-031-31097-3

This Palgrave Macmillan imprint is published by the registered company Springer Nature Switzerland AG.
The registered company address is: Gewerbestrasse 11, 6330 Cham, Switzerland

Paper in this product is recyclable.

To the memory of Dragan Tepavcevic; to Emma and Biljana

Preface

Being a fresh migrant meant being different from the majority. This was my first impression as a teenage migrant from collapsing Yugoslavia in Moscow in the 1990s. It was much harder for me to study compared to my local peers, because I had to start from scratch by learning the language and customs. Similarly, in the absence of stable employment and clear immigrant regulations in the turbulent post-Soviet labor market, my parents founded a small engineering company. The business secured our chances for regular income and legal and economic integration into the chaotic early post-Soviet community. As a student, I also worked part-time as a journalist and helped my parents with the administration of our family business. This constituted my first experience as an entrepreneur. Later on, when I moved to Hungary for my postgraduate studies, I founded another family business with my partner. This entrepreneurship allowed me to continue balancing my academic work with parenting.

As a newly minted PhD, female migrant, and mother, I faced challenges in finding a sustainable income in academia. This led to seeking stability through family entrepreneurship. I utilized my academic background in international and comparative political economy as a guide in my entrepreneurial endeavors as a researcher and consultant. Some results of these efforts were published in peer-review journals, and these publications served as valuable references for the present book. Among other positions, I also worked as a researcher for a Budapest-based entrepreneurship incubator, where I observed with disappointment that these disciplines were entirely unnoticed in courses offered to entrepreneurs. This short book highlights my combined academic and migrant entrepreneurial journey through various economic and social systems in the European Union. It is also an attempt in building the theoretical and empirical bridges between studies in comparative political economy, entrepreneurship, and migrations. I hope that both scholars and entrepreneurs will benefit from this book.

Kőszeg, Hungary Sanja Tepavcevic

Acknowledgments

The research and writing processes sometimes appear as a long and lonely journey that would be unbearable without the support of many people and institutions. Part of the research in Hungary was supported by my alma mater CEU Global Teaching Fellowship (2016–2017) and another by the RFBR, Grant No. 19-511-23001 (2019–2022). The research in Austria was supported by the Institute of Advanced Studies Koszeg (iASK) research fellowship grant in 2020. My special thanks go to the former CEU Pro-Rector, Liviu Matei; Director of iASK's Polanyi Center, Jody Jensen; and Research Fellow of CEU Department of Environmental Sciences and Policy and my colleague from Budapest-based International Association Dialogue, Irina Molodikova. I owe access to the most up-to-date literature to iASK (the most devoted) librarians Eszter Takacs and Henrietta Doka. For sharing their works and experiences, I deeply appreciate my senior colleagues from a wide range of institutes across Europe: Julius Horvath (CEU), Istvan Abel (BGE), Laszlo Karvalics (iASK), Sergey Ryazantsev and Marina Khramova (Moscow Institute of International Relations, or MGIMO, and Institute of Demography, Russian Academy of Sciences), Larysa Tamilina (iASK), and Csaba Weiner (Institute of World Economics, Hungarian Academy of Sciences). I also owe my passion for comparative political economy to the faculty and student members of Central European University's Political Economy Research Group, where I was a member in the period between 2008 and 2016. I thank the editors of *Migration and Ethnic Themes* and *Review of Economic Theory and Policy* journals for their advice on how to reuse my previously published work.

I would like to thank Palgrave Macmillan editor Wyndham Hacket Pain and two anonymous reviewers, whose comments on the proposal for this monograph helped me sharpen my research approach and strengthen my argument.

Thanks to immense technical support from Pasha and Minja, the formatting process went relatively smoothly. I also want to take this opportunity to thank a truly British member of my family, my loving Masha Milovanovich for her help in making this monograph clear and readable. My special thanks also go to all of the anonymous respondents in formal and informal conversations, participants of focus groups and online surveys in Austria, Spain, and Hungary, who shared their migrant and entrepreneurial experiences and insights, providing me with wider empirical perspectives related to entrepreneurship in emigration. I also want to thank Rita Hasanova, Irina Tatarenko, Anastasia Mitrofanova, Marina Strachenko, Oxana Bosovich, Ilya and Nastya Kruk. Finally, without moral support and friendship of Zara, Yura, Natalia, Oleg, Ilya, Natasha, Anna, Vadym, and Dima, this journey would have been much harder.

Contents

About the Author

Sanja Tepavcevic (Tepavcsevics Szonja), PhD, is Adjunct Professor in International Studies Master Program at the Department of Modern Philology and Social Sciences of the University of Pannonia, and Associate Researcher of the Institute of Advanced Studies Koszeg, Hungary. She has held positions at the Central European University, Budapest, the Budapest Business University, and Eötvös Lóránd University. She is a member of the Budapest-based NGO Dialogue and was an external associate of the Croatian Institute of European and Globalization Studies. She holds a diploma in Journalism from Moscow State University, an MA in International Relations and European Studies, and a PhD in Political Science from the CEU. Her research includes Russian and Ukrainian foreign policy, post-Soviet migrations and immigrant entrepreneurship, and foreign economic policies of former Yugoslav states and V4 countries. Her publications include articles in high-ranked peer-reviewed journals, for example, "In the Bear's Shadow? Russia's Image and Its Influence on Investments of Russian Companies in Post-Socialist Europe," published in 2018 by the *Journal of East-West Business*, policy reports, book reviews, chapter in edited book, and comments in media.

Abbreviations

CEE	Central and Eastern Europe
CME	Coordinated Market Economy
DME	Investment Dependent Market Economy
EU	European Union
FSU	Former Soviet Union
LME	Liberal Market Economy
MME	Mediterranean or Mixed Market Economy
MNC	Multinational Corporation
SME	Small and Medium Enterprises
USSR	Union of Soviet Socialist Republics
VoC	Varieties of Capitalism
VoIR	Varieties of Immigration Regimes

List of Tables

PART I

CHAPTER 1

Varieties of Post-Soviet Migrations and Varieties of Entrepreneurship in Varieties of Capitalism

Abstract This chapter investigates the relationship between immigrant entrepreneurship and the concept of Varieties of Capitalism in comparative political economy. It highlights the importance of combining these areas of study, particularly for scholars and policymakers dealing with migration issues. The chapter delves into the theory that the market economy and immigrant integration are intertwined and interrelated. The research proposes that the degree of immigrant integration is tightly tied to the form of market economy in place.

Keywords Post-Soviet migrations • Institutional variety • Entrepreneurship variety • Migrant entrepreneurship

1.1 Introduction: Varieties of Post-Soviet Migrations and Immigrant Entrepreneurship

The demise of the world's former second superpower, the Soviet Union, and the fall of the Socialist bloc led to a transformation of economic systems, characterized by the collapse of socialist political regimes and the establishment of market institutions in their countries' remnants (Aslund, 2007; Gustafson, 1999). The impact of this system change on Soviet citizens was studied by Turaeva (2022), who found that the early post-Soviet

S. Tepavcevic, *Diversity of Migrant Entrepreneurship in Varieties of European Capitalism*,
https://doi.org/10.1007/978-3-031-31097-3_1

period was characterized by chaos, *"bespredel,"* or *"beshabashnie vremena."* This was due to low state salaries, forcing many to take on additional jobs in the evenings, even professionals such as doctors and teachers. In places like Tashkent, where state salaries could not cover basic needs, professionals were forced to supplement their income by working as taxi drivers. This lack of income created difficulties in meeting basic needs, let alone financing long-term expenses like weddings, funerals, or property purchases. Furthermore, in economies dominated by the informal sector, cash was the dominant mode of exchange (Turaeva, 2022).

On the one hand, the collapse of communist-era economic institutions initially created an economic vacuum in which Soviet populations built their livelihoods on available resources, mostly informal networks known as *blat* (Rodgers et al., 2018), and the need to belong to a particular social circle in order to be economically successful (Remennick, 2012; Turaeva, 2022). As a result, numerous types and forms of entrepreneurship emerged (Kshetri, 2009). People, who became entrepreneurs during these transformations, were seen as quasi-entrepreneurs, who capitalized on the opportunities created by the disintegration of the Soviet system and the turbulence of the early post-Soviet transition (Gustafson, 1999). Many of the early post-Soviet enterprises characterized as unproductive and destructive (Sauka, 2008) turned out to be negative for the socioeconomic environment of the post-Soviet republics.

On the other hand, this socioeconomic vacuum triggered a massive wave of emigration from the newly independent post-Soviet republics, which peaked in the first half of the 1990s. This wave consisted of post-Soviet Jews, whose numbers reached over one million, in Israel alone, representing 20 percent of the total Israeli population (Mesch & Czamanski, 1997). Other large post-Soviet communities, including post-Soviet Jews, Armenians, and Germans, emigrated to Germany, the United States (USA), and Canada (Aron, 1991; Remennick, 2012; Shvarts, 2010). From the mid-1990s, waves of migration from and within the former Soviet Union (SU) included Chechens, Russians, Kazakhs, and Ukrainians (Molodikova, 2019; Ryazantsev, 2015). The earliest of these waves coincided with the 1998 financial crisis and the large capital outflow from the post-Soviet countries. At the same time, the former Soviet republics have remained among the top twenty sending countries over the last three decades (*IOM Report 2018*). In 2019, the number of Russian citizens living outside Russia alone numbered ten million, while migrations via Ukraine, Kazakhstan, and Uzbekistan were among the largest European emigration corridors (*IOM Report 2020*).

Subsequently, many of these post-Soviet immigrants set up businesses in the host countries and became entrepreneurs with migrant backgrounds. Two of the most striking examples are the co-founder of Google, Sergey Brin (Leadem, 2017), and the former owner of the British football club, Chelsea, Russian oligarch Roman Abramovich (Kuznetsov, 2011), both of whom have made international headlines. Similarly, many post-Soviet immigrants founded their businesses operating across the European Union (EU) (Tepavcevic et al., 2020). By 2015, post-Soviet citizens became one of the largest immigrant groups in the EU (Ryazantsev, 2015). Because of this striking and mass character, post-Soviet immigrant entrepreneurship has attracted academic interest at the outer limits of several fields of study, including post-Soviet migrations, the economics of emerging markets, outward foreign direct investment (OFDI) from the former Soviet republics, and the broader fields of immigrant entrepreneurship and studies of business. In studying post-Soviet immigrant businesses in Canada, for example, Shvarts (2010) noted that "the important intellectual issue, is how did immigrants who grew up most of their lives in a state-controlled communist system where entrepreneurship was forbidden, learn to become so adept at starting businesses in a market economy" (Shvarts, 2010, p. ii).

Other scholarly research on post-Soviet immigrant entrepreneurship represents a number of single case studies. They range from the creation of Ukrainian enclaves in Italian cities (Matricano & Sorenttino, 2014) and the entrepreneurship of Russian women in the Norwegian countryside (Munkejord, 2017) to the entrepreneurship of Russian-speaking communities in several European countries as well as Asian and African states (Byford, 2012; Johansson, 2006; Okulov, 2007; Ryazantsev, 2017; Tepavcevic, 2017). These studies have demonstrated that the entrepreneurship of post-Soviet immigrants in European countries varies between the local and mainstream economies, depending mainly on the length of their stay in a host country. Some studies also noted that the cultural and ethnic heritage of post-Soviet migrants, most notably Chechens, hindered their economic and legal integration in the EU (Molodikova, 2019). In contrast to most studies that examined Russian language businesses in Asian and African countries, Ryazantsev (2017) found that post-Soviet immigrants had few opportunities for cultural and social integration, and therefore they organized, as Ryazantsev puts it, Russian-language migrant economies and even Russian villages that emerged in Cambodia, Thailand, Vietnam, and Liberia.

Similarly, most studies recognize the relationship between the timing of emigration and the type and form of immigrant entrepreneurship. For example, Shvarts (2010) points out that Russians who immigrated to Canada in the late 1980s without financial resources were engaged in ethnic businesses, while most relatively wealthy post-Soviet emigrants moved to North American and EU countries after 2000 where they established businesses operating in the regular economies of the receiving countries. Moreover, Ryazantsev et al. (2018) found three major waves of post-Soviet emigration and recognized certain types of migrants in each of them. For example, from 1991 to 1998, they found refugees who emigrated mainly to Israel, Germany, and the USA, and post-Soviet gray-traders, who settled in Poland, Turkey, or the United Arab Emirates. The next wave peaked in the early 2000s, before the global financial crisis, and it divided into labor emigrants and post-Soviet oligarchs. The latter invested their usually "gray" new earnings abroad and tried to legalize them, and the main direction of emigration was Great Britain and the offshore zones. The last wave of post-Soviet emigration (before the 2022 Russian-Ukrainian war triggered the largest migration since World War II) peaked after the global financial crisis. In 2013, negotiations about Ukraine's Association agreement with the EU evolved around disagreements between pro-European and pro-Russian Ukrainian political factions. With the involvement of the EU and Russia, disagreements soon escalated into political crisis and violent conflict paired with Russia's annexation of Crimea from Ukraine in 2014. This move tremendously worsened Russia-EU relations, resulting in mutual sanctions and an economic crisis in Russia, creating a new wave of post-Soviet migrations to Europe. At the same time, the migration crisis that peaked in the summer of 2015 bringing thousands of refugees from the Middle East and Afghanistan to Europe deepened existing disagreements between the EU members over immigrant quotas. Disagreements escalated further and led Great Britain to hold a Brexit referendum in 2016, which made both Brexit and immigration significant issues within the European Union (EU). Simultaneously, this EU internal political crisis is also reflected in the EU relations with Russia and Ukraine. Following long-term disputes among member states, in 2018, the EU introduced a free-visa regime with Ukraine, which led to an increase in transnational migration and generated a new way of emigration from Ukraine to the EU. As a result, this wave consisted of middle-class representatives, pensioners, transmigrants, and small and medium-sized legal business owners, as argued by Ryazantsev et al. (2018) and Tepavcevic et al. (2020).

With the full-scale invasion of the Russian army in Ukraine that began in February 2022, emigration from Ukraine reached over seven million in less than a year and from Russia between three million and five million, respectively. This has generated the largest migration wave since World War II. This escalation of conflict in Europe put the EU into the most pessimistic scenario concerning migration. Ukrainian citizens, primarily women, including highly skilled professionals, children, and to some extent the elderly, have left primarily for the EU, seeking refuge from the violence and destruction. In response, the EU activated a Temporary Protection Directive allowing them residence permits, access to the labor market, housing, medical assistance, and access to education for children (European Commission, 2023). As a result, by March 2023, the estimated number of Ukrainian refugees had surpassed four million across the EU. Poland and Germany emerged as the primary receiving countries, with the Czech Republic, Bulgaria, Romania, Italy, and Spain also serving as significant host countries (Union, 2023).

Simultaneously, Russian citizens, predominantly middle-class professionals, businesspersons, scientists, and young political and social activists escaped due to increased danger from political and ideological prosecutions, economic uncertainty, and mobilization. Their emigration to the EU was constrained by COVID-19-related travel restrictions, the absence of direct flights to EU countries, and visa regimes. As a result, Russian army's invasion in Ukraine and the related increasing political and social repressions in Russia prompted Russian citizens' emigration to countries that did not require entry visas, including post-Soviet Georgia, Armenia, and Kazakhstan, Serbia, and Montenegro in Europe, and Turkey (Zavadskaya, 2022). At the same time, only small percentage of Russian citizens went to the EU countries, mainly the Baltic States and Germany (Kamalov et al., 2022).

To curtail the Russian governments ability to wage the war against Ukraine, the EU has so far adapted eleven sanction packages. They included the suspension of the EU's Visa Facilitation Agreement on September 9, 2022, as well as the suspension of Russia's status of Most-Favored-Nation under World Trade Organization (WTO) framework, imposing export and import bans on a wide range of high-technologies and products (Commission, 2022). These sanctions put an end to all investments of Russian state-owned companies and to some private trade-related businesses led by Russian citizens in the EU. Therefore, while both Ukrainian and Russian emigration are driven by the same source of threat, there are striking differences in their demographic characteristics, geography of emigration, and migration statuses. These developments have already begun to shape the emergence of distinct Ukrainian and Russian migrant communities. However, between 1991 and 2022, these communities overlapped, at least within the EU.

The studies that form the debate on entrepreneurship among immigrants from the post-Soviet space thus provide a complex theory on this phenomenon. Indeed, the nature and geography of post-Soviet immigrant entrepreneurship depends on the timing of emigration from the FSU homelands. While in the late years of the USSR's existence, Soviet citizens usually immigrated without financial resources and, after arriving in the host countries, became necessity entrepreneurs setting up ethnic enterprises. From the late 1990s onward, the majority of post-Soviet emigrants moved to the countries with advanced market economies with significant financial sources. As a result, they remain active in the regular economies of the receiving countries.

This theory has two limitations. Firstly, it is based on the motives and timing of emigration, and secondly, while it acknowledges the influence of institutions in the receiving country on post-Soviet entrepreneurship, the institutional aspect of entrepreneurship in the receiving countries is under-researched. To date, there is a lack of comparative studies on the relationship between immigrant entrepreneurship in different institutional settings, especially in the EU. As González-Ferrer and Moreno-Fuentes (2017) pointed out, these gaps need to be addressed in future research.

This chapter delves into the limitations of the traditional neoclassical economic model for understanding migration patterns, which only considers the distribution of capital and labor. Instead, it underscores the need to consider a multitude of other factors such as history, sociology, and politics to comprehend the complex nature of migration.

This short book aims to provide insights into one of fundamental socio-economic questions: what is the role of host countries institutions in immigrant entrepreneurship? Thus, the book investigates the relationship between cultural heritage, informal institutions, and formal institutions in the immigration and integration of post-Soviet migrants in different institutional settings across the EU. Specifically, it seeks to answer the question of how immigrant entrepreneurship contributes to the integration of post-Soviet citizens in the EU. To address these questions, this book brings together theories from different disciplines. The first is comparative political economy, which focuses on the interactions between formal political and economic and informal socio-cultural institutions. The second is the broader discipline of applied sciences—the study of business, management, and entrepreneurship. The third is migration studies, which is a significant intersection of the social sciences—sociology, international relations, politics, public policy, law, and social anthropology. In the last two decades, the Varieties of Capitalism (VoC) paradigm, first proposed by Hall and Soskice (2001), has become the dominant analytical paradigm in comparative political economy (Ebner, 2015; Feldmann, 2019). By first placing firms at the center of analysis (Hall & Soskice, 2001; Schneider, 2013), VoC successfully integrated business and management studies with the study of institutions in comparative political economy. VoC has also been successfully applied in studies of governance (Walter & Zhang, 2012), policy reform (Bohle & Greskovits, 2012), and more recently in studies of entrepreneurship (Dilli et al., 2018; Herrmann, 2019).

The monograph aims to broaden the discussion on the VoC approach by exploring its connection to immigrant entrepreneurship. The book is divided into three parts. Part I consists of two chapters. The first chapter reviews the literature on the interaction between institutions and entrepreneurship and integrates the Varieties of Capitalism (VoC) approach with immigrant entrepreneurship and immigration regimes. This overview forms the basis for the analytical framework that links VoC and immigrant entrepreneurship. Chapter 2 clarifies the key concepts used in the book, explains the rationale behind the selection of case studies, and describes the methods of data collection and analysis. Part II, the empirical part of the book, consists of three chapters that analyze the relationship between the economic model and the immigration regime in three selected EU Member States. Each chapter examines the types, forms, sectors, and role of entrepreneurship in the integration of post-Soviet immigrants in one of the selected EU countries. Part III includes two chapters. Chapter 6 provides a comparative analysis of the findings from the empirical chapters, highlighting similarities and differences in the role of entrepreneurship in the integration of post-Soviet immigrants in the three EU Member States. The final chapter summarizes the findings and their implications for further research.

1.2 The Diversity of Institutions in Varieties of Capitalism: Origins and Extensions of the VoC Paradigm

Institutions, the "man-made rules of the game" (North, 1991), are at the core of any system, be it a small business, a community, a state or a global order. Scott (2008) has divided institutions into six different categories, starting with the macro level—world system and societal institutions—followed by the meso level—organizational field and organizational population—and concluding with the micro-level organization and organizational subsystems. Thornton et al. (2012) coin the term "institutional logic" and define their seven ideal types: Family, Religion, State, Market, Profession, Corporation, and Community Logic. According to these definitions, institutions can be described as either informal or formal. Informal institutions include traditions, customs, moral values, religious beliefs, and all other norms of behavior that have withstood the test of time (Pejovich, 1999), culture (Boettke & Coyne, 2009; Kontos, 2003), or religion and a social class (Audretsch et al., 2013). Formal institutions include the rules of governance and the form of government, constitutions, treaties, laws, and regulations (North, 1991). Institutions are also crucial to the economic activities of large communities where it is otherwise impossible to rely on reputation and thus be perfectly informed (Milgrom et al., 1990). Hall and Soskice (2001) have proposed the appropriate framework for these analyses in the edited volume titled Varieties of Capitalism.

Varieties of Capitalism—VoC for short—brought together the disciplines of comparative political economy, business studies, and political science in a dynamic framework of the analyzing institutions. VoC originally focused on the analysis of firms, and Hall and Soskice (2001) distinguished between two contrasting models of advanced market economies. These are liberal market economies (LMEs) and coordinated market economies (CMEs). The third model Hall and Soskice (Hall & Soskice, 2001) recognize is that of mixed market economies (MMEs) because it has mixed characteristics of LMEs and CMEs. Institutional complementarity—the most important VoC concept—is the central feature of these institutional models. In Hall and Soskice's original VoC, these complementarities relate to five spheres of corporate relations. The first sphere is industrial relations, which refers to wages and the working conditions, with LMEs representing company wages and short-term contracts, and CMEs functioning through union-regulated wages and long-term contracts. The second sphere is vocational education and training, where LMEs are characterized by the demand for general skills, while CMEs are characterized by the demand for specific skills. As a result, in LMEs the enterprises provide relevant training for employees, while in CMEs, they do it in cooperation with trade unions and educational institutions.

The third sphere of institutional complementarity is corporate governance, that is, access to finance and return investment. In this sphere, LMEs are characterized by the pursuit of high and immediate profits, while CMEs are focused on long-term, distributed profits through cooperation. In the fourth sphere—inter-firm relations—LMEs are characterized by strong inter-firm competition for both suppliers and clients, while in CMEs firms coordinate with other firms and cooperate on both supply and customers. The final sphere of institutional complementarity is firms' relations with their employees. In LMEs, as in the other four spheres, the relationships are based on competitive demand, supply, and fulfillment of mostly task-related contractual terms, while in CMEs they are mostly long-term contracts based on trust and mutual development. MMEs appear in the middle between two institutional contrasts, LMEs and CMEs. Indeed, MMEs usually offer moderate levels of social protection with high investments in poverty alleviation and pension provision. Additionally, in MMEs external shareholders are not well protected and venture capital from national investors is scarce. National spending for education is also limited. The firms in MMEs have a comparative advantage in low-cost production (Molina & Rhodes, 2007).

The transformation of Central and Eastern European economies has led economists to examine their development and extend the VoC approach to the analysis of these countries. Highlighting the liberal character of the state and the dependent nature of the economy, King (2007) labeled the VoC in Central and Eastern Europe (CEE) as "liberal dependent post-communist capitalism" (LDPC). LDPC, represented in King's study by Hungary and Poland, was characterized by dependence on foreign investors for the provision of credit and the organization of inter-firm relations, the weakness of the labor market, dysfunctional education systems, and LME-type relations between firms and workers. From a comparative political economy perspective, the Czech Republic, Hungary, Poland, and Slovakia were considered four cases of the same basic variant of the market economy, with very similar socioeconomic institutions, characterized mainly by this heavy reliance on foreign direct investment (FDI). Because of this dependency on FDI, Nölke and Vliegenthart

(2009) have coined them dependent market economies (DMEs). Table 1.1 summarizes the characteristics of four major VoC models.

Streeck and Thelen (2005) criticized the VoC approach, pointing out its limitations in considering institutions as static rather than dynamic entities. They argued that institutional change is a constant phenomenon and that economic policy institutions worldwide have undergone a process of liberalization, which they consider inevitable. Despite this criticism, the VoC approach proved fruitful in the study of political systems. For example, Bohle and Greskovits (2012) utilized the VoC approach to analyze market economies in post-socialist Europe and placed the state at the center of their analysis. They proposed a deeper understanding of the diversity of emerging market economies based on Karl Polanyi's (1944) concept of the social and political embeddedness of economic activities. Bohle and Greskovits (2012) distinguished between three models of market economies: the neoliberal model represented by the post-Soviet Baltic states, the embedded neoliberalism model embodied by the DME (Feldmann, 2019), and the neo-corporatist model represented by Slovenia. Being found in four significant Central and Eastern European member states, DME model attracted more scholarly attention than its neoliberal and neo-corporatist counterparts. As a result, the VoC approach recognizes four variants of market economies in the EU: the liberal market economy (LME) represented by Ireland; the coordinated market economy (CME) represented by Germany, the Netherlands, Austria, the Scandinavian countries, and Slovenia; the DME represented by the Visegrad Four group; and the neo-corporatist market represented by Slovenia.

After the inclusion of post-socialist Europe, VoC debates have expanded to emerging and developing countries and even to the international level. Following Hall and Soskice (2001), Hancke et al. (2007), and Hancké (2009), several volumes have dealt with VoC models and their regional diversity in Latin America and Asia. Similar to Hall and Soskice (2001), Schneider (2013) takes a firm-centered approach to the Latin American capitalisms, conceptualizing them as hierarchical market economies (HMEs), of which Chile is a striking example. He contrasts these types of non-OECD market economies with network market economies (NMEs), which are based on trust and implicit long-term contracts or norms, as opposed to CMEs, which are based on bargaining. This type of market economy is exemplified by Japan and Taiwan respectively, according to Schneider (2013). Similarly, Walter and Zhang (2012) develop an overarching framework for understanding the politics of institutional stability

Table 1.1 VoC models of market economies and their major characteristics

Market economy model/country group	*LME—USA, UK, Ireland*	*MME—Italy, Spain, France, Portugal*	*DME—Poland, Czech Republic, Slovakia, Hungary*	*CME—Germany, Austria, Sweden, Netherlands*
Characteristics	In LMEs, competition prevails as labor and financial markets are deregulated, so that shareholder capital is available to firms in the short run, while labor is mobile. This deregulated institutional environment leads firms to engage with their business partners in a highly competitive way, thereby facilitating radical innovations (Dilli et al., 2018; Hall & Soskice, 2001)	MMEs provide moderate levels of social protection with high investments into poverty alleviation and pensions. External shareholders are not well protected, and venture capital from national investors is hardly available. Similarly, national expenditure for education is limited. This gives firms in MMEs a comparative advantage in low-cost production—with the exception of some niche markets, for example, furniture or fashion, where Italian firms compete on incremental innovations and design (Dilli et al., 2018; Molina & Rhodes, 2007)	DMEs provide a comparative advantage in the assembly and production of relatively complex and durable consumer goods. These comparative advantages have been based on institutional complementarities that combine low labor costs and a skilled population with substantial knowledge of medium-level technologies. Contrary to CMEs, employers in DMEs are unwilling to bear the additional costs of on-the-job training for inexperienced young workers. Similarly, the second most important source of finance, domestic bank lending is dominated by transnational companies (Hancké et al., 2007; Nölke & Vliegenthart, 2009)	In CMEs, economic actors often engage with each other on the basis of nonmarket relationships. The institutions regulating financial and labor markets tie shareholders as well as workforces to "their" firm. This, in turn, leads firms to cooperate closely with their financiers and employees, which makes the institutional environment conducive to incremental (technological) innovation (Dilli et al., 2018; Hall & Soskice, 2001)

and change by focusing on governance in East and Southeast Asia through three sets of variables, namely coalitions of interest, state action and capacity, and policy discourses.

Following the VoC approach, Whitley (2003) took the two initially opposing models of market economies at the international level and recognized that national institutions also compete at this higher level. Through this competition, the national types of market economies produce two types of international business environments—IBEs. The first, which is similar to LMEs, is prevalent in the international business environment. It promotes formalized business services of the US type—accounting, consulting, law—and, according to Whitley, serves US hegemony. Examples include the World Trade Organization (WTO) and North American Free Trade Agreement (NAFTA). Another variation of IBE resembles CMEs and promotes the coordination of business relations and services. An example of such an IBE is the EU, which counterbalances US global hegemony. At an international level, the CME-like IBE thus represents—to use Karl Polanyi's (1944) term—a "countermovement" to the dominant LME IBE.

Ebner (2015, p. 2) affirms the importance and increasing influence of VoC in comparative political economy and warns that this "should not result in a misled understanding of regional varieties of capitalism as relatively autonomous units of operation," but rather as "components of a multilevel and multi-scalar structure of co-evolving actor constellations and strategic relationships." He therefore argues for further research into "the internal diversity of overlapping institutional settings within and across the confines of national settings" (Ebner, 2015, p. 2). Following this suggestion, this book examines post-Soviet entrepreneurship in three continental European models of market economies.

1.3 Varieties of Entrepreneurship in Varieties of Capitalism

The concept of entrepreneurship has been central to economic debates and has been defined by several famous economists of the twentieth century. Joseph Schumpeter (1934) defined it as "creative disruption." George Douglas Howard Cole and Raymond Postgate (1946) described it as "the use of one factor of production by other factors of production to create economic goods" (Hughes, 1983). Peter Drucker (1986) expanded the definition to encompass both practice and discipline, emphasizing its close link to innovation as often approached with a "step-by-step" mentality, focusing on addressing specific opportunities and needs. According to Drucker (1986), this practical approach, as opposed to a rigid one, allows for flexibility and continuous improvement in any society, economy, industry, public service, or business. Drucker (1986, p. 255) also introduced the concept of "entrepreneurial society" in which he envisioned entrepreneurship as "an integral life-sustaining activity in our organizations, our economy, our society," meaning that entrepreneurship extends to all types of organizations.

Nevertheless, in business and management studies and in the social sciences, the term entrepreneurship predominantly refers to complex economic activities. Boettke and Coyne (2009), for example, point out that entrepreneurship can manifest itself in various ways. They include buying low and selling high, discovering and disseminating lower-cost technologies in production, introducing new products, learning how to better deliver goods and services to customers at lower cost, and creating new ways to alert potential buyers to the availability and attractiveness of new products are all entrepreneurial acts in the marketplace. According to Boettke and Coyne (2009), the defining characteristic of entrepreneurship is the pursuit of bettering one's own situation through beneficial exchange with others.

Entrepreneurship has two main forms in terms of its impact on economics: rapid change and incremental change. The first form, rapid change, is rooted in Schumpeter's (1934) theory of economic development and the idea that there is no equilibrium in the market system. The second form, incremental change, is conceptualized by the Austrian school of economics represented by Hayek, Mises, and Kirzner. Both theories agree that the entrepreneur is the cause of disequilibrium, but the causes differ. In Schumpeter's theory, the entrepreneur causes disequilibrium through innovative intervention and seizing opportunities, while in the Austrian school, entrepreneurship is a constant, subjective approach to economic and social phenomena. These two perspectives on entrepreneurship align with two opposite models of the free market: Schumpeter's entrepreneur embodies the functioning of firms in LMEs, while the Austrian School's entrepreneur represents the functioning of firms in CMEs (Vaz-Curado & Mueller, 2019).

In terms of its impact on the wider environment in which it operates, entrepreneurship can take three further forms, namely productive, unproductive, and destructive. In general, productive entrepreneurship refers to any activity that contributes directly or indirectly to the net output of the economy or to the ability to generate additional output (Baumol, 1993) and is thus by definition legal. Conversely, the legal but unproductive form of entrepreneurship is usually associated with economic activities that benefit their initiators, but do not generate additional output. Finally, illegal forms of wealth-enforcing activities that produce negative net outputs such as rent-seeking are considered destructive entrepreneurship (Sauka, 2008). By adding institutions and entrepreneurship to economic growth, Bosma et al. (2018) demonstrate that productive entrepreneurship contributes to economic growth and that in their set of proxies for institutional quality, financial stability, small government, and perceived start-up skills are the most important predictors of a productive entrepreneurship. These forms of entrepreneurship are summarized in Table 1.2.

The relationship between entrepreneurship and the institutional environment is reciprocal. The institutional environment has a profound impact on entrepreneurship and, at the same time, entrepreneurship shapes the institutional environment. Boettke and Coyne (2009) explain this connection by emphasizing the influence of the institutional environment on entrepreneurial opportunities. They explain that the quality of the institutional environment affects the opportunities available to entrepreneurs, and if the institutions generate a net benefit for productive activities, such as innovation and arbitrage, entrepreneurs will take advantage of these opportunities, leading to wealth creation. Conversely, if the benefits of unproductive activities, such as rent-seeking and crime, are relatively high, entrepreneurs will pursue those opportunities.

Furthermore, Su et al. (2017) analyzed the business and management literature to identify the institutions that impact entrepreneurship at macro, meso, and micro levels. At the macro level, they found a focus on market freedom, legal institutions for entrepreneurship, and resource

Table 1.2 Forms of entrepreneurship related to innovations and net output

Forms of entrepreneurship related to innovations	*Forms of entrepreneurship related to net output*
Schumpeterian—disruption, radical change	Productive—producing additional output
Austrian school—constant incremental change	Unproductive—benefiting initiators without producing additional output
	Destructive—producing negative net outputs

availability. At the meso level, they discovered the influence of community institutions and organization field institutions, and at the micro level, institutionalized practices and organizational level legitimacy. As a result, Su et al. (2017) noted that business and management literature has a lack of agreement on the theoretical foundation of institutions and limited research on the interaction between different institutions. This gap was partly addressed by Henrekson and Rosenberg (2000), who compared the impact of national institutions on entrepreneurship in Sweden and the USA. They found that despite substantial government support and research, Sweden lagged behind the USA in science-based entrepreneurship due to factors such as lower returns on human capital investment and insufficient incentives within the university system.

However, the comprehensive application of the VoC approach in the field of entrepreneurship has received growing attention in recent scholarly discussions. The works of Herrmann (2019) and Herrmann (2020) have revealed the variation in barriers to entrepreneurial ventures across different regions of Europe. For instance, in the UK, there is a high number of ideas and entrepreneurs, but limited access to a skilled workforce hampers their ability to establish successful firms. Conversely, in Germany, starting a business is challenging, but those that do often become successful global players. Dilli et al. (2018) conducted a macro-level analysis of the sources of entrepreneurship and found that the forms of entrepreneurship are correlated with the types of market economies defined by the VoC. Their findings demonstrate that entrepreneurship resources and forms range from Schumpeterian entrepreneurship, characterized by risk-taking, radical innovations, and a focus on high corporate growth, typically found in LMEs, to non-Schumpeterian entrepreneurship, characterized by risk-avoidance, imitation, and a lack of focus on corporate growth, typically found in CMEs. The results of their analysis also indicate that each type of market economy generates a specific level of innovative entrepreneurship, as summarized in Table 1.3.

Therefore, while recognizing the mutual influence between entrepreneurship and national institutions, business and management studies, as Herrmann (2019) pointed out, tend to have a "radical change bias." This bias is characterized by a focus on radically innovative ventures that develop new technology-based products, leading to strong corporate growth but also to a higher risk of failure. The radically innovative ventures have emerged particularly frequently in Silicon Valley. The success stories of Silicon Valley entrepreneurs are frequently depicted in

Table 1.3 Varieties of entrepreneurship in VoC concerning innovation

VoC economic model	*LME*	*CME*	*MME*	*DME (EME)*[a]
Variety of entrepreneurship concerning innovation	Deregulated, radical innovation—the benchmark of innovation	The second most innovative, increasingly Schumpeterian, while well-regulated institutions also contribute to incremental innovations	"Entrepreneurs in MMEs outperform entrepreneurs in all other economies in the extent to which they set up low-tech ventures, but hardly set up any high-tech or medium-high-tech ventures compared to their counterparts in other economies"[b]	Entrepreneurs in DMEs perform better in setting up medium-low-tech ventures than entrepreneurs in CME and MME; simultaneously, they are outperformed by their counterparts in LMEs and CMEs in setting up high-tech ventures

[a]Dilli et al. (2018) use EME (that stands for Eastern European market economies) as the synonym for DME
[b]Dilli et al. (2018, p. 310)

mainstream movies in the USA (S. Anderson & Platzer, 2006). Similarly, while the field of immigrant entrepreneurship is an important area of study in migration studies, it lacks the VoC-framed debates. To bridge this gap, the next section will review the major postulates proposed by scholars of immigrant entrepreneurship.

1.4 (Unrecognized Varieties of) Immigrant Entrepreneurship

(Im)migrant entrepreneurship differs from traditional entrepreneurship in that it is undertaken by migrants of specific socio-cultural or ethnic backgrounds or by the people of migrant origin. In contrast to local population, migrants often face limited access to the host country's labor market due to structural, statistical and sometimes even taste-based discrimination (Marchand & Siegel, 2015; Zhou, 2004). Therefore, in contrast to business studies, which focus on entrepreneurship mostly as a mean of innovation and economic growth, the debates about immigrant entrepreneurship tend to be on the social aspect of entrepreneurship, rather than its role in innovation and economic growth. Immigrant entrepreneurship is particularly prevalent in large cities, which are geographic focal points for goods and services markets, housing markets, labor markets, capital markets, and innovation markets (Marchand & Siegel, 2015; Sassen, 1991). Migrant entrepreneurs also play a significant role in the small-and-medium enterprises (SME) sector of cities in countries with advanced economies, though with varying degrees of success (Sahin et al., 2013).

The relationship between migration and entrepreneurship has been traditionally explored from the perspective of the impact of migration on the cultural and economic landscapes of traditional host countries in North America and Western Europe. Literature on immigrant entrepreneurship has often focused on immigrants who engage in ethnic enterprises, as they may have competitive advantages over the native population (Light, 1984). For example, Portes (1997) found that entrepreneurship of the Cuban diaspora in Miami served goals and means of itself: thus, Portes characterized it as "ethnic entrepreneurship." Additionally, the scholars focusing on immigrant entrepreneurship pointed out that immigrant entrepreneurship can be driven by a combination of positive factors related to the place of destination and negative factors related to the place of origin (Lee, 1966). Positive factors in the place of destination include demand for ethnic products and/or services and negative factors in the country of origin, such as limited career and professional opportunities (Orozco, 2008) and investment opportunities in host countries (Marchand & Siegel, 2015; Rath, 2006). Similarly, negative factors related to the place of origin included getting better payment for the same job and better professional opportunities than available in home countries (Portes, 1997; Waldinger, 2009), but also possibilities for getting support for the development of innovations as driving motives from low-to-middle income countries to those with high income (Graham, 2013).

Moreover, Sahin et al. (2006, 2013) focused on immigrant entrepreneurship in the Netherlands and found that various ethnic groups had distinct business attitudes based on their cultural background. Similarly, examining migrant entrepreneurship in the context of the EU enlargement, Baycan and Nijkamp (2007, p. 16) noticed that despite the significant contribution of migrants to the labor markets of the EU and their entrepreneurship's positive impact on socioeconomic development,

> their participation rate in the labour market is on the whole lower than that of the native population, certain categories of immigrant labour force—women, young people and elderly workers—face specific difficulties in entering the labour market, and they are often more exposed to unemployment than the native population.

Overall, scholars have found that immigrant entrepreneurship is driven by a combination of push and pull factors and that cultural background can influence business attitudes and success. However, immigrants often face barriers to entering the labor market, which can push them toward entrepreneurship as a means of economic survival. In turn, the literature on immigrant entrepreneurship in advanced market economies suggests two main propositions. Firstly, immigrants from developing countries often migrate to countries with advanced market economies in search of better living standards and investment opportunities. Due to limited access to the receiving country's labor market, they often turn to entrepreneurship as a means of integration and prosperity. Secondly, to further integrate and succeed in the receiving country, many immigrants invest their savings and utilize the demand from their ethnic communities to engage in forms of ethnic enterprise, catering to the needs of their ethnic group.

Scholars of immigrant entrepreneurship have often compared the policies and impact of immigration in Europe and North America. For example, Sahin et al. (2013) noted that if Europe does not address current economic trends, its share of world production will decline as emerging Asian economies catch up. They argue that Europe needs more entrepreneurship to strengthen its economic position. According to their research, approximately 20 million enterprises in the European Economic Space (including Switzerland) all together employ more than 122 million people. The majority of these enterprises are very small, with 93 percent having 1 employee, 6 percent being small with 10 employees, less than 1 percent being medium-sized with approximately 50 employees, and less than 1 percent being large with 250 or more employees. This is in contrast to the average American company, which employs nineteen people. As a result, SME's make up 46 percent of total employment in the USA, while they represent over 66 percent of total employment in Europe (Sahin et al., 2013).

Several studies on immigrant entrepreneurship in post-Socialist countries in Central and Eastern Europe have found that immigrant-owned businesses are increasingly becoming a part of these countries' mainstream economies (Tepavcevic et al., 2020). For example, Brzozowski and Pedziwiatr (2016) found that entrepreneurship among immigrants of various origins in Lesser Poland primarily operates in the mainstream market. These studies also highlight a difference in the integration of immigrant entrepreneurs between advanced economies in the USA and Western Europe and post-socialist countries in Central Europe. In the former immigrant-owned businesses tend to primarily serve their own ethnic communities or other immigrants, while in the latter they are increasingly becoming part of the mainstream market.

Furthermore, the debate on immigrant entrepreneurship has expanded to show the detailed complexity of migration and entrepreneurial processes. Prior to the COVID-19 pandemic, significant advancements in communication and transportation and their lowered costs have drastically increased socioeconomic mobility and enabled migrations for education, work, network, and collaboration between countries and their markets. For example, Ren and Liu (2015) found that Chinese immigrant entrepreneurs in Singapore use mutually reinforcing strategies of transnationalism—the trend of combining immigrant status and experience to build business and create advantage by bridging sending and receiving countries—and integration to accumulate social and economic resources in both China and Singapore. This idea has further been developed into the analytical framework of simultaneous embeddedness proposed by Nazareno et al. (2018). This analytical framework consists of two sets of three-leveled factors, one in the home country and another in the host country, focusing on how three-leveled factors in the home country interact with those in the host country: at the micro level, pre-migration statuses may affect their business performance in the host country. At the meso level, socioeconomic conditions in the home country (e.g. the expansion of middle-class families, the labor shortage, and the favorable government policies) may affect the local labor market in the host country.

At the macro level, politico-institutional factors in the home country may enable or constrain transnational entrepreneurial ambition in the host country. Additionally, when examining female immigrant entrepreneurship specifically in Vienna, Dunnecker and Cakir (2016) found that women entrepreneurs of immigrant origin in Vienna perceive their geographic mobility not only as the boundary-drawing marker, but also as a qualification and a mean of social mobility. Therefore, immigrants perceive their geographical mobility as a significant qualification and a means of social mobility and utilize it in building transnationally operating businesses in their host and home countries.

Further, the literature on technology and international business history highlights the crucial role of immigrant entrepreneurs in innovation and technology transfer. Scholars such as Graham (2013) emphasize the positive impact that immigrant entrepreneurs have on job creation and technology exchange in their host societies. Additionally, the efficiency of bureaucracy is considered a crucial factor affecting innovation and entrepreneurial activities (Acs et al., 2014). Anderson and Platzer (2006) provide evidence of this by showing that immigrant entrepreneurs founded several major high-technology companies in the USA, such as eBay, Yahoo, and Google. These examples illustrate the Schumpeterian type of immigrant entrepreneurship and its impact on innovation and technology transfer. However, it is also highlighted that the efficiency of bureaucracy in the host country plays a significant role in the success of these processes.

1.5 (Undebated Varieties of) Immigration and Integration Policies

Finally, these debates about immigrant entrepreneurship are closely linked to those on migration, and they provide two general types of empirically grounded propositions about factors influencing migrants' economic integration into the receiving societies. The first type of propositions focuses on political factors, such as national migration policies of receiving countries. For example, as Platt et al. (2021) point out, "immigrants' employment chances are negatively associated with national levels of expenditure on welfare benefits but positively associated with policies facilitating immigrant access to social security." They also find that labor market rigidity negatively affects immigrants' occupational attainment, but there is little evidence that policies aimed at supporting the transferability of immigrants' qualifications promote their occupational success. Thus, their results suggest that anti-discrimination policies are important for immigrant economic integration.

The literature on immigrant integration highlights two socio-cultural factors that affect their integration in receiving countries and societies. Firstly, social capital is linked to a sense of community and "foreignness" (Kontos, 2003; Portes & Sensenbrenner, 1993). Strong communication within the immigrant community enhances social capital (Aldrich &

Zimmer, 1986) and creates a pool of resources that can foster business and increase the likelihood of success. Secondly, ethnic entrepreneurship provides a way for immigrants to establish a collective identity in the host country and access resources (Kontos, 2003). Discrimination faced by a community can lead to increased solidarity and support within the community (Kontos, 2003). In this process, the use of the immigrants' native language can strengthen ethnic ties and solidify the collective identity of the community.

In sum, the connection between immigration, the integration of immigrants in host societies, and the impact of immigrant entrepreneurship on these processes is a topic of ongoing discussion. Political and economic conditions in the host country, the level of social capital within immigrant communities, and the extent of ethnic entrepreneurship solidarity have all been recognized as crucial factors affecting the success of immigrant entrepreneurship. Despite this, the role of the institutional context in these discussions has yet to be fully explored. Based on a review of existing literature, including post-Soviet perspectives, it would be worthwhile to propose a hypothesis that can be tested through empirical research in subsequent chapters.

1.6 The Missing Debates in the VoC Paradigm, Missing the VoC Approach in Migration and Immigrant Entrepreneurship Debates: Varieties of Immigrant Entrepreneurship Framework

In summary, the literature on the VoC has overlooked migration studies and the immigrant entrepreneurship field, despite their relevance. Similarly, migration studies overlooked the analytical power of VoC taxonomy. Recently Boucher and Gest's (2018) analysis of immigration regimes has bridged some aspects of these two wide debates. They define immigration regimes as policies and their results that collectively reflect the admission and settlement of foreign-born people over time. Like Hall and Soskice (2001) in VoC, and Dilli et al. (2018) in varieties of entrepreneurship, Boucher and Gest (2018) use the liberal model of market economy as a benchmark for their taxonomy. In their classification, the opposite of liberal immigration regime is the EU's "Free Movement" model and its subclassifications. Interestingly, their sub-type of "Extra-Union Regime" coincides with MMEs, while the subtype of "Intra-Union Regime" refers to traditional CME countries, Austria, Germany, Netherlands, and Denmark among the EU members, and Norway and Switzerland among the European economic area members. However, this classification overlooks a cluster specific to Central Eastern European countries, which has been mentioned in literature on immigrant entrepreneurship (Brzozowski & Pedziwiatr, 2016; Tepavcevic et al., 2020). To address this gap, a comprehensive analysis of the Hungarian immigration regime is provided in Chap. 5.

1.7 Conclusions: Theoretical Axes and Factors Under Scrutiny

As reviewed in the literature on immigrant entrepreneurship, there are two main theoretical perspectives that appear to be in opposition to each other: the necessity theory and the opportunity theory. The necessity theory posits that immigrants from developing countries often turn to entrepreneurship as a means of improving their standard of living and accessing investment opportunities not available in their home countries due to limited access to the receiving country's labor market. On the other hand, the opportunity theory argues that immigrants engage in entrepreneurship because of advantages they have, such as their savings and the demand for goods and services within their ethnic communities, which they can tap into by starting an ethnic enterprise.

The second theoretical axis in immigrant entrepreneurship literature concerns the type of embeddedness of immigrant entrepreneurship in the receiving country's economy. This axis is based on the dichotomy between ethnic entrepreneurship and mainstream economy entrepreneurship. This dichotomy is present not only in immigrant entrepreneurship literature but also in the subfield of post-Soviet immigrant entrepreneurship. The dichotomy closely relates to the factor of time of emigration. For example, the theory of post-Soviet immigrant entrepreneurs posits that the type and geography of post-Soviet immigrant entrepreneurship depends on the time of emigration from the home countries of the FSU: in the early 1990s, Soviet citizens usually emigrated without financial resources, and in the receiving countries, they became necessity entrepreneurs who created ethnic businesses. On the contrary, in the late 1990s and on, most post-Soviet emigrants moved to countries with advanced market economies with substantial financial resources. As a result, they operate in the mainstream economies of receiving countries. Institutional change in the receiving countries frequently debated in the VoC literature is, therefore, crucial aspect in study of immigrant entrepreneurship.

In addition to the VoC paradigm and migration debates, other complementing institutional factors contribute to the understanding of immigrant entrepreneurship. Among them are migrants' cultural background, level, and aspect of integration into the host society, transnational mobility as a qualification, and migrants' role in transferring innovations and technology. These factors influence the ways in which immigrant entrepreneurs conduct their businesses, from family and community ties to business attitudes, from social integration to geographical mobility. The efficiency of bureaucracy also plays a critical role in the transfer of innovations and technology between sending and receiving countries. It remains to be seen how these factors affect post-Soviet entrepreneurs in the EU and whether the effects are consistent across different receiving countries.

The next chapter provides a detailed analysis of major concepts, a description of the research design and the logic behind selecting Austria, Spain, and Hungary as country cases and how they may have affected the experiences of post-Soviet immigrant entrepreneurs. Empirical chapters that follow Chap. 2 will aim to identify patterns and similarities among post-Soviet immigrant entrepreneurs in the EU and understand how the factors mentioned above have influenced their experiences and success in each country. The cultural background, level of integration, transnational mobility, role in innovation and technology transfer, and the impact of the type of market economy will also be examined in each country. Overall, this research will contribute toward a better understanding of the dynamics and challenges of immigrant entrepreneurship in the EU, specifically concerning post-Soviet immigrant entrepreneurship.

References

Acs, Z., Auito, E., & Szerb, L. (2014). *Global Entrepreneurship and Development Index 2014.* Springer.

Aldrich, H., & Zimmer, C. (1986). Entrepreneurship through Social Networks. In *The Art and Science of Entrepreneurship* (pp. 3–23). Ballinger Publishing Company.

Anderson, S., & Platzer, M. (2006). *American Made: The Impact of Immigrant Entrepreneurs and Professionals on U.S. Competitiveness.* National Venture Capital Association.

Aron, L. (1991). *Preparing America for the Wave of Russian Immigrants.*
Aslund, A. (2007). *How Capitalism was Built. The Transformation of Central and Eastern Europe, Russia and Central Asia.* Cambridge University Press.
Audretsch, D., Bönte, W., & Tamvada, J. (2013). Religion, Social Class, and Entrepreneurial Choice. *Journal of Business Venturing, 28*(6), 774–789.
Baumol, W. (1993). Formal Entrepreneurship Theory in Economics: Existence and Bounds. *Journal of Business Venturing, 8*(3), 197–210.
Baycan, T., & Nijkamp, P. (2007). *Migrant Entrepreneurship in a Diverse Europe: In Search of Sustainable Development.*
Boettke, P., & Coyne, C. (2009). *Context Matters: Institutions and Entrepreneurship.* https://doi.org/10.1561/0300000018
Bohle, D., & Greskovits, B. (2012). *Capitalist Diversity on Europe's Periphery.* Cornell University Press.
Bosma, N., Concent, J., Sanders, M. W., & Stam, E. (2018). Institutions, Entrepreneurship, and Economic Growth in Europe. *Small Business Economics, 51*(4), 483–499.
Boucher, A., & Gest, J. (2018). *Crossroads: Comparative Immigration Regimes in a World of Demographic Change.* Cambridge University Press.
Brzozowski, J., & Pedziwiatr, K. (2016). *Pushed to the Mainstream Market: The Case of Immigrant Entrepreneurs in Lesser Poland.* Paper presented at the Cross-Border Migration and its Implications for the Central European Area, Bratislava.
Byford, A. (2012). The Russian Diaspora in International Relations: "Compatriots" in Britain. *Europe-Asia Studies, 64*(4), 715–735.
Cole, G. D. H., & Postgate, R. (1946). *The Common People 1746–1946.* Methuen.
Commission, E. (2022). EU Sanctions Against Russia Following the Invasion of Ukraine. https://eu-solidarity-ukraine.ec.europa.eu/eu-sanctions-against-russia-following-invasion-ukraine_en
Dilli, S., Elert, N., & Herrmann, A. (2018). Varieties of Entrepreneurship: Exploring the Institutional Foundations of Different Entrepreneurship Types through 'Varieties-of-Capitalism' Arguments. *Small Business Economics, 51*(2), 293–320.
Drucker, P. F. (1986). *Innovation and Entrepreneurship: Practice and Principles.* Harper & Row.
Dunnecker, P., & Cakir, A. (2016). Female Migrant Entrepreneurs in Vienna: Mobility and its Embeddedness. *Österreichische Zeitschrift für Soziologie, 41*, 97–113.
Ebner, A. (2015). Editorial: Exploring Regional Varieties of Capitalism. *Regional Studies, 50*(1), 3–6.
European Commission, M. a. H. A. (2023). Migration Management: Welcoming Refugees from Ukraine. https://home-affairs.ec.europa.eu/policies/migration-and-asylum/migration-management/migration-management-welcoming-refugees-ukraine_en

Feldmann, M. (2019). Global Varieties of Capitalism. *World Politics, 71*(1), 162–196.

González-Ferrer, A., & Moreno-Fuentes, F. J. (2017). Back to the Suitcase? Emigration during the Great Recession in Spain. *South European Society and Politics, 22*(4), 447–471.

Graham, L. (2013). *Lonely Ideas. Can Russia Compete?* The MIT Press.

Gustafson, T. (1999). *Capitalism—Russian Style*. Cambridge University Press.

Hall, P. A., & Soskice, D. (2001). *Varieties of Capitalism: The Institutional Foundations of Comparative Advantage*. Oxford University Press.

Hancké, B. (2009). *Debating Varieties of Capitalism: A Reader*. Oxford University Press.

Hancké, B., Rhodes, M., & Thatcher, M. (2007). *Beyond Varieties of Capitalism: Conflict, Contradiction, and Complementarities in the European Economy*. Oxford University Press.

Henrekson, M., & Rosenberg, N. (2000). Designing Efficient Institutions for Science-Based Entrepreneurship: Lesson from the US and Sweden. *Journal of Technology Transfer, 26*(3), 207–231.

Herrmann, A. (2019). A Plea for Varieties of Entrepreneurship. *Small Business Economics, 52*(2), 331–343.

Herrmann, A. (2020). On the Institutional Foundations of the Varieties of Entrepreneurship in Europe. In *The Entrepreneurial Society. International Studies in Entrepreneurship* (Vol. 44, pp. 331–343). Springer.

Hughes, J. (1983). Arthur Cole and Entrepreneurial History. *Business and Economic History, 12*, 331–343.

IOM Report 2018. (2018).

IOM Report 2020. (2020).

Johansson, L. (2006). *International Business Operations of Companies with Russian Involvement in Southwestern Finland*.

Kamalov, E., Kostenko, V., Sergeeva, I., & Zavadskaya, M. (2022). *Russia's 2022 Anti-War Exodus: The Attitudes and Expectations of Russian Migrants*.

King, L. P. (2007). Central European Capitalism in Comparative Perspective. In *Beyond Varieties of Capitalism: Conflict, Contradiction and Complementarities in the European Economy* (pp. 307–327). Oxford University Press.

Kontos, M. (2003). Self-employment Policies and Migrants' Entrepreneurship in Germany. *Entrepreneurship and Regional Development, 15*(2), 119–135.

Kshetri, N. (2009). Entrepreneurship in Post-Socialist Economies: A Typology and Institutional Contexts for Market Entrepreneurship. *Journal of International Entrepreneurship, 7*(3), 236–259.

Kuznetsov, A. (2011). *Outward FDI from Russia and its Policy Context*.

Leadem, R. (2017). The Immigrant Entrepreneurs Behind Major American Companies. *www.entrepreneur.com*. https://www.entrepreneur.com/article/288687

Lee, E. S. (1966). A Theory of Migration. *Demography, 3*(1), 47–57.
Light, I. (1984). Immigrant and Ethnic Enterprise in North America. *Ethnic and Racial Studies, 7*(2), 195–216.
Marchand, K., & Siegel, M. (2015). *World Migration Report 2015: Immigrant Entrepreneurship in Cities—Background Paper.*
Matricano, D., & Sorenttino, M. (2014). Ukrainian Entrepreneurs in Italy: Factors Influencing the Creation of Ethnic Ventures. *Journal of Innovation and Entrepreneurship, 3*, 10.
Mesch, G., & Czamanski, D. (1997). Occupational Closure and Immigrant Entrepreneurship: Russian Jews in Israel. *The Journal of Socio-Economics, 26*(6), 597–610.
Milgrom, P., North, D., & Weingast, B. (1990). The Role of Institutions in the Revival of Trade: The Law Merchant, Private Judges, and the Champagne Fairs. *Economics and Politics, 2*(1), 1–23.
Molina, O., & Rhodes, M. (2007). The Political Economy of Adjustment in Mixed Market Economies: A Study of Spain and Italy. In *Beyond Varieties of Capitalism* (pp. 223–252). Oxford University Press.
Molodikova, I. (2019). Muslim Refugees from Russia: Do the Chechens Bring Their Own "aul" from Chechnya to the EU? In *In Muslim Minorities and the Refugee Crisis in Europe. Narratives and Policy Responses* (p. 339). SGH.
Munkejord, M. C. (2017). Local and Transnational Networking among Female Immigrant Entrepreneurs in Peripheral Rural Contexts: Russian Female Entrepreneurs in Norway. *European Urban and Regional Studies, 24*(1), 7–20.
Nazareno, J., Zhou, M., & You, T. (2018). Global Dynamics of Immigrant Entrepreneurship. Changing Trends, Ethnonational Variations, and Reconceptualizations. *International Journal of Entrepreneurial Behavior & Research, 25*(5), 780–800.
Nölke, A., & Vliegenthart, A. (2009). Enlarging the Varieties of Capitalism: The Emergence of Dependent Market Economies in East Central Europe. *World Politics, 61*(4), 670–702.
North, D. C. (1991). Institutions. *The Journal of Economic Perspectives, 5*(1), 97–112.
Okulov, J. (2007). Russian Immigrant Entrepreneurship in Finland. [In Russian.]. In *In Immigrants, Multiculturalism and the World of Work* (pp. 51–80). University of Kuopio.
Orozco, M. (2008). *Tasting Identity: Trends in Migrant Demand for Home-Country Goods.*
Pejovich, S. (1999). The Effects of the Interaction of Formal and Informal Institutions on Social Stability and Economic Development. *Journal of Markets and Morality, 2*(2), 164–181.
Platt, L., Polavieja, J., & Radl, J. (2021). Which Integration Policies Work? The Heterogeneous Impact of National Institutions on Immigrants' Labor Market

Attainment in Europe. *International Migration Review, 56*. https://doi.org/10.1177/01979183211032677

Polanyi, K. (1944). *The Great Transformation: The Political and Economic Origins of Our Time*. Beacon Press.

Portes, A. (1997). *Globalization from Below: The Rise of Transnational Communities*. Princeton University.

Portes, A., & Sensenbrenner, J. (1993). Embeddedness and Immigration: Notes on the Social Determinants of Economic Action. *American Journal of Sociology, 98*, 1320–1350.

Rath, J. (2006). *Entrepreneurship among Migrants and Returnees: Creating New Opportunities*, Turin.

Remennick, L. (2012). *Russian Jews on Three Continents. Identity, Integration, and Conflict*. Transaction Publisher.

Ren, N., & Liu, H. (2015). Traversing between Transnationalism and Integration: Dual Embeddedness of New Chinese Immigrant Entrepreneurs in Singapore. *Asian and Pacific Migration Journal, 24*(3), 298–326.

Rodgers, P., Vershanina, N., Williams, C., & Theodorakopoulos, N. (2018). Leveraging Symbolic Capital: The Use of Blat Networks Across Transnational Spaces. *Global Networks, 19*(1), 119–136.

Ryazantsev, S. (2015). The Modern Russian-Speaking Communities in the World: Formation, Assimilation and Adaptation in Host Societies. *Mediterranean Journal of Social Sciences, 6*(3S4). https://doi.org/10.5901/mjss.2015.v6n3s4p155

Ryazantsev, S. (2017). "Russian-Russian" Economy as Mechanism of the Integration of Russian-Speaking Migrants in the Receiving Countries. *Journal of Economics, 25*(1), 122–136.

Ryazantsev, S., Pismennaya, E., Lukyantsev, A., Sivoplyasova, S., & Khramova, M. (2018). Modern Emigration from Russia and Formation of Russian-Speaking Communities Abroad (In Russian). *World Economy and International Relations, 62*(6), 93–107.

Sahin, M., Nijkamp, P., & Baycan-Levent, T. (2006). Migrant Entrepreneurship from the Perspective of Cultural Diversity. *Series Research Memoranda, 16*.

Sahin, M., Nijkamp, P., & Suzuki, S. (2013). Survival of the Fittest among Migrant Entrepreneurs. *A Study on Differences in the Efficiency Performance of Migrant Entrepreneurs in Amsterdam by Means of Data Envelopment Analysis.*

Sassen, S. (1991). *The Global City*. Princeton University Press.

Sauka, A. (2008). Productive, Unproductive and Destructive Entrepreneurship: A Theoretical and Empirical Exploration. https://doi.org/10.2139/ssrn.1147811

Schneider, B. R. (2013). *Hierarchical Capitalism in Latin America: Business, Labor, and the Challenges of Equitable Development*. Cambridge University Press.

Schumpeter, J. (1934). *The Theory of Economic Development*. Harvard University Press.

Scott, W. R. (2008). Approaching Adulthood: The Maturing of Institutional Theory. *Theory and Society. Special Issue on Theorizing Institutions: Current Approaches and Debates, 37*(5), 427–442.

Shvarts, A. (2010). Elite Entrepreneurs from the Former Soviet Union: How They Made Their Millions. PhD dissertation.

Streeck, W., & Thelen, K. (2005). *Beyond Continuity: Institute of Advanced Political Economies.* Oxford University Press.

Su, J., Zhai, Q., & Karlsson, T. (2017). Beyond Red Tape and Fools: Institutional Theory in Entrepreneurship Research, 1992–2014. *Entrepreneurship Theory and Practice, 41*(4), 505–531.

Tepavcevic, S. (2017). Immigrant Entrepreneurship in the Post-Socialist Countries of the European Union: Motives and Patterns of Entrepreneurship of Post-Soviet Immigrants in Hungary. *Migration and Ethnic Themes, 1*, 65–92.

Tepavcevic, S., Molodikova, I., & Ryazantsev, S. (2020). Post-Soviet Russian-Language Migration, Investment, and Entrepreneurship in Eastern and Central Europe (for Example of Hungary, Austria, and the Czech Republic). *Today and Tomorrow of the Russian Economy [In Russian], 99–100*, 5–22.

Thornton, P., Lounsbury, M., & Ocasio, W. (2012). *The Institutional Logics Perspective: A New Approach to Culture, Structure, and Process.* Oxford University Press.

Turaeva, R. (2022). Measuring Humans Through Money: Anthropology of Debt in Post-Soviet Economies. *Social Lives of Debts: Ethnographies from Post-Soviet and Post-socialist Economies, 6*(1).

Union, C. o. t. E. (2023). Infographic—Refugees from Ukraine in the EU. https://www.consilium.europa.eu/en/infographics/ukraine-refugees-eu/

Vaz-Curado, F., & Mueller, A. (2019). The Concept of Entrepreneur of Schumpeter in Comparison to Kirzner. *Interdisciplinary Journal of Philosophy Law and Economics, 7*(3), 613–642.

Waldinger, R. (2009). Beyond Transnationalism: An Alternative Perspective on Immigrants' Homeland Connections. In *Oxford Handbook of the Politics of International Relations* (pp. 74–102). Oxford University Press.

Walter, A., & Zhang, X. (2012). *East Asian Capitalism: Diversity, Continuity, and Change.* Oxford University Press.

Whitley, R. (2003). Changing Transnational Institutions and Management of International Business. In *Globalization and Institutions* (pp. 108–133). Edward Elgar.

Zavadskaya, M. (2022). Anti-war Wave of Emigration: Should I Stay or Should I Go? Riddle website: https://ridl.io/anti-war-wave-of-nbsp-emigration-should-i-nbsp-stay-or-nbsp-should-i-nbsp-go/

Zhou, M. (2004). Revising Ethnic Entrepreneurship: Convergencies, Controversies, and Conceptual Advancements. *International Migration Review, 38*(3), 1040–1074.

CHAPTER 2

Operationalizing Post-Soviet Immigrant Entrepreneurship in VoC: Concepts, Research Design, and Methods of Inquiry

Abstract The present chapter has four goals. Firstly, it unpacks the key concepts used in this short book to offer a model for the evaluation of immigrant entrepreneurship. Secondly, it bridges the concept of Varieties of Capitalism (VoC) with the concept of immigration regime in the European Union (EU) context offering the new concept of Varieties of Immigration Regimes (VoIR). Thirdly, the chapter reveals the logic behind the selection of Austria, Spain, and Hungary as country case studies and delves into methods of inquiry. The chapter also offers a detailed description of the methods of inquiry applied in this study.

Keywords Post-Soviet migrants • Institutions • Immigrant entrepreneurship • Migrant entrepreneurs • Capitalist variety • Immigration regimes

2.1 Central Concepts in the Study and Their Use

The analysis presented in this study revolves around eleven central concepts: Post-Soviet migrants, immigrant entrepreneurship, immigrant entrepreneurs, the Varieties of Capitalism (VoC) approach, home and host countries, formal and informal institutions, (Varieties of) immigration regimes, and integration. These concepts may be defined differently

S. Tepavcevic, *Diversity of Migrant Entrepreneurship in Varieties of European Capitalism*,
https://doi.org/10.1007/978-3-031-31097-3_2

depending on the discipline, but in order to synthesize theoretical foundations from comparative political economy, business studies, and migration studies in country-and-immigrant-group-focused case studies, the definitions of these concepts are operationalized in their general meanings.

The central concept of this analysis is the post-Soviet (im)migrants, referring to individuals who were born in countries that were formally part of the Soviet Union and whose primary language of communication is Russian or are bilingual. The concept of post-Soviets has been defined differently by scholars in the field of migration studies. While Heleniak (2017) considered all individuals from former socialist countries as post-Soviet, grouping them based on their political and social background, previous works by the author focused on individuals who were citizens of the former Soviet Union (Tepavcevic, 2017; Tepavcevic et al., 2020). Additionally, until 2014, many host countries' official statistics, such as those in Germany, Israel, and Hungary, classified citizens of post-Soviet countries as "citizens of the former USSR" long after the dissolution of the Soviet Union (Ryazantsev et al., 2018). The Soviet geographical origins and a native-level knowledge of the Russian language place post-Soviet emigrants within a coherent and often ethnically diverse migrant group (Tepavcevic, 2020). The multinational and multicultural nature of the former Soviet Union, the concept of Soviet people, subsequent national and ethnic minority issues, and nation-building efforts in the vast post-Soviet territories prompted some scholars to focus exclusively on emigrants from particular former Soviet republics. However, as both studies and practice demonstrate, post-Soviet political nations frequently do not coincide with the self-identifications of many of their citizens. They usually share Russian as a common language of communication or *lingua franca*, and the experience of political-economic and social transformations across post-Soviet space and consequent shared cognitive frameworks prompted by the educational and social institutions make post-Soviet people a relatively coherent unit of analysis. In previous works, it has been noted that

> [n]ationally and ethnically defined as Ukrainians, Russians, Jews, or Kazakhs, their narratives have demonstrated that their networks create culturally distinctive post-Soviet immigrant communities: most of them referred to themselves as being Soviet: "Soviet children/childhood", "our—Soviet", "we—the Soviet people" ...The vast majority of them share the mentality—similar worldviews mostly based on the experience of poverty, and certain

> social equality in such poverty—experienced in home countries in the Soviet past. For most of them, immigration to the West meant the search for better living standards and opportunities. Still, after they migrated, they tend to look for their compatriots and other former Soviet citizens to comfort themselves in host environments, where they have extensively used the Russian language both in the social and economic spheres of their lives. (Tepavcevic, 2021, p. 150)

Thus, post-Soviet migrants resemble Anderson's (1991) concept of "imagined community": once formally institutionalized political nation, the term "post-Soviet (im)migrants" refers to former Soviet citizens and those who were born in countries-remnants of the Soviet Union and whose major language of communication is Russian or are bilingual.

Secondly, entrepreneurship is defined as "the capacity and willingness to develop, organize, and manage a business venture along with any of its risks in order to make a profit" (Business Dictionary) and as "the act of improving one's own situation by engaging in beneficial, wealth-enhancing exchange with others" (Boettke & Coyne, 2009). It involves interactions between institutions of various forms and operating at different levels. Relatedly, an immigrant entrepreneur is defined as a foreign-born, self-employed, officially registered person, regardless of her/his citizenship status in the receiving country. Fourthly, the terms "country of origin," "sending country," and "home country" are used interchangeably, as are the terms "country of destination," "receiving country," and "host country." Fifthly, immigrant entrepreneurship is defined as the effort by immigrants in receiving countries to either maintain or improve their own situation through beneficial exchange with others. Finally, "post-Soviet immigrant entrepreneurs" refers to individuals (and their economic activities) originating from the countries of the former Soviet Union who are self-employed or operate their own firms.

The classification of post-Soviet immigrant entrepreneurship in this monograph stems from the following evaluation model summarized in Table 2.1.

The evaluation of post-Soviet immigrant entrepreneurship is based on three main criteria. The first criterion assesses their position in the host country's market, evaluated by the size and sector of their entrepreneurial activities. The second criterion examines the relationship of their entrepreneurship to the post-Soviet immigrant community, categorizing it as an "enclave" business, a business serving the mainstream market with

Table 2.1 Criteria for classification of post-Soviet immigrant entrepreneurship

Classification criteria	*Description*	*Details*
Place in host country's market	Size and industry of entrepreneurship	Micro, small, medium, large size and industry (construction, energy, tourism, IT)
Role in post-Soviet immigrant community	Extent of supply and demand from the post-Soviet immigrant community	(a) "enclave" business, (b) enclave-supplied mainstream business; (c) post-Soviet-led mainstream-oriented; (d) post-Soviet-owned mainstream and/or globally-oriented
Role in immigrants' integration	Entrepreneurship fulfilling either one or more aspects of integration	Aspects of integration—legal, social, economic, or mixture of two or more

supplies from the post-Soviet community, or a business integrated into the global market. The third criterion explores the role of entrepreneurship in the immigrants' integration into the host country, considering whether it provides legal, social, and/or economic integration. Defining the size of immigrant business also proved the context-dependent question requiring certain standardization. Thus, for the analytical purposes, the post-Soviet businesses were defined as follows. Businesses were defined as micro when employed up to five persons and small when they employed between ten and twenty persons; companies employing between twenty and eighty persons were defined as medium businesses. Finally, businesses with over eighty employees were regarded as large.

The central concept of the Varieties of Capitalism (VoC) analytical paradigm plays a crucial role in the analysis, classifying countries based on their economic model and the functioning of their institutions. In the context of post-Soviet immigrant entrepreneurship, the VoC taxonomy serves as a starting point for discussion. Institutions defined as the rules and models of human behavior are also the key in the analysis. They shape behavior at macro, meso, and micro levels and vary across geographies. In this book, institutions are defined as systems. Formal institutions such as political, economic, and legal—as opposed to earlier discussed informal ones—are operationalized through the VoC framework.

The ninth concept discussed in the book is the complex notion of immigration regimes. According to Boucher and Gest (2018), an immigration regime refers to "the migration policies and their outcomes that collectively reflect the admission and settlement of foreign-born people over time." Therefore, immigration regimes also represent formal institutions. Throughout the analysis, this definition is maintained. Usually, all immigration and immigrant integration regimes stem from one of two basic principles rooted in Roman law: *jus sanguinis*, which is based on ethnic or cultural ties and is prevalent in most of continental Europe and characterized by a coordinated economic model; or *jus soli*, which is based on birth in a country or length of stay and is the cornerstone of the constitutions of traditional immigration countries and embodies liberal market economies. Thus, the relationship between economic models in the VoC paradigm and immigration regimes is a central aspect of the analysis.

Still, countries that share similar immigration experiences can fall under different immigration regimes. According to Halse (2022), each country's immigration policies are shaped by its past experiences with colonization, immigration, political ideologies, and economy. Based on EU migration regulation, Boucher and Gest (2018) categorize the EU as a "Free Movement" immigration regime, but this characterization has been met with criticism from migration scholars. They argue that the EU's restrictive immigration policies toward non-EU citizens, particularly those who are unskilled or low-skilled, contradict this characterization (Baubock, 2006; Baycan & Nijkamp, 2006; Zimmerman, 2005). The debates and criticisms surrounding the EU immigration regime in the contexts of some EU members are discussed in detail in Chaps. 3, 4, and 5 of the monograph.

Boucher and Gest (2018) identify two sub-regimes within the EU: the Extra-Union regime and the Intra-Union regime. The Extra-Union regime is seen in Western and Southern European countries and is characterized by accepting language-speaking immigrants from similar countries. The Intra-Union regime, on the other hand, is typical in countries like those of continental Europe, Scandinavia, and the Netherlands. Hungary's immigration regime is not included in this categorization and is instead analyzed using the DME VoC model, which compares it with the Czech Republic and Slovakia. These EU immigration sub-regimes can be considered "Varieties of Immigration Regimes" or VoIR.

The tenth concept discussed in the book is the integration of immigrants. In the European Union (EU), the process of immigrant integration is evaluated in four key areas: employment, education, social inclusion, and active citizenship (European Parliament, 2016). This monograph takes an opposite angle assessing integration through the narratives of post-Soviet immigrants on their immigrant entrepreneurship. The concept of third-country nationals (TCNs) is also relevant and is defined according to EU regulations as

> [A]ny person who is not a citizen of the European Union within the meaning of Art. 20(1) Treaty on the Functioning of the European Union (TFEU) and who is not a person enjoying the European Union right to free movement, as defined in Art. 2(5) Regulation (EU) 2016/399. (Schengen Borders Code)

In other words, TCNs are individuals who are not citizens of the EU or those who do not have the right to free movement within the EU. Overall, the study investigates the relationship between post-Soviet immigration, entrepreneurship, and integration in the EU. It offers a classification of immigrant entrepreneurship based on the combination of these factors and their impact on the integration of post-Soviet immigrants in three EU member states. The analysis incorporates the concept of embeddedness, introduced by Karl Polanyi (1944), which views the economy as closely tied to the social context in which it operates. As a result, this study approaches entrepreneurship not just as an isolated economic activity, as is commonly studied in business and management, but rather as an integral part of larger social processes, particularly immigration and immigrant integration.

2.2 The Logic of Country Case Selection

The classification of immigration regimes is critical in forming the analytical framework that links the established VoC theoretical paradigm to immigrant entrepreneurship. It serves as a standard for evaluating immigrant entrepreneurship in other models of market economies and immigration regimes, drawing on lessons learned from the study of immigrant entrepreneurship in liberal market economies (LMEs). As noted by Weinar (2018), migration studies have traditionally had a limited scope, focusing primarily on Western liberal democratic countries of destination and heavily influenced by American scholarship. This has resulted in a narrow emphasis on themes specific to the pluralist conception of politics in the USA and Western Europe and a neglect of other regions, including Central and Eastern Europe in the EU. Nevertheless, the study of migration politics has evolved, with new avenues of research emerging, such as comparative studies of citizenship regimes (Brubacker, 1992) and integration regimes (Castles, 1995).

Therefore, it is crucial to thoroughly research immigrant entrepreneurship in European coordinated market economies (CMEs) and Mediterranean or mixed market economies (MMEs). Among the former, Switzerland, Germany, and the Netherlands have received the most attention from scholars, while Austria, despite having a significant and growing immigrant population, has received less attention. To address this imbalance, the first empirical study on post-Soviet immigrant entrepreneurship in this monograph was conducted in Austria. In 2019, Austria had a population of 16 percent immigrants, and this number reached 20 percent by 2021 ("Statistics Austria—Migration," 2021–2022).

The research on immigrant entrepreneurship in MMEs has predominantly focused on Italy and France, but has generally neglected Spain despite its similar size and growing immigrant population. To address this empirical gap, Chap. 4 of this monograph examines post-Soviet immigrant entrepreneurship in Spain. While there have been some studies on immigrant entrepreneurship in Central and Eastern Europe (CEE), they do not link it with the models of CEE economies. Four CEE countries were previously characterized as dependent market economies (DMEs) in the VoC paradigm. However, their immigration regimes have not been thoroughly examined, requiring further analysis and classification. To address this gap, Chap. 5 utilizes existing studies and new examples of post-Soviet immigrant entrepreneurship in Hungary to classify the immigration regime and provide a fresh perspective on immigrant entrepreneurship in DME.

2.3 Methods and Strategies of Inquiry

The research aimed at understanding and systemizing the post-Soviet immigrants' perceptions and interpretations of the role of entrepreneurship in their personal immigration and integration experiences. Therefore, the data analyzed in this book is predominantly qualitative and was collected in the period between 2013 and 2022 in multiple phases. The first step involved researching and analyzing scholarly literature related to institutions and economic development, Soviet history, post-Soviet transformations, Soviet and post-Soviet migrations, immigrant entrepreneurship, and post-Soviet immigrant entrepreneurship. The sources were searched in both English and Russian, and criteria such as relevance to the topic, the type of publication, and the geographical territory covered were applied. Statistical data on the number of post-Soviet immigrants in Austria was obtained mostly from Austria's government reports, while information for Spain and Hungary was gathered also from International Organization of Migration's (IOM) country profiles, Organisation for Economic Co-operation and Development (OECD), and Eurostat.

The second phase of research comprised online sources. In conducting online research, it is important to explain the researcher's positionality. There has been ongoing debate among ethnographers since 2014 regarding the nature of digital ethnography and its relationship to traditional ethnography. Ethnographers are divided into two camps: those who view digital ethnography as a distinct field and those who view it as an upgrade of classical ethnography methods (Caliandro, 2014; Wesch, 2009). The first camp, led by prominent ethnographer Robert Kozinets, believes that digital ethnography is "native to the digital environment" (Kozinets, 2015) and utilizes tools such as crowdsourcing and social network analysis (Kozinets, 2015). They argue that digital ethnography is significantly different from traditional ethnography, dealing not just with words but also with a range of digital artifacts, including images, audio files, and website creations. As such, they believe it deserves a new name—Netnography—and recognition as a separate discipline.

On the other hand, some ethnographers view digital ethnography as a contemporary upgrade of classical ethnography, incorporating the new technologies and methods while retaining the core principles of traditional ethnography, rather than a separate discipline (Kovacevic-Bielicki & Pejovic, 2020; Miller, 2018; Pink et al., 2016; Skageby, 2011). Instead, they propose that it is simply a contemporary upgrade of classical qualitative research methods. According to them, digital ethnography is a qualitative approach to data collection in digital communities. The debate continues but the author's position on this issue should be clearly stated in any research conducted in this field. Despite recognizing the advantages of both the aforementioned approaches in specific contexts, the author positions herself as an online ethnographer—as opposed to "netnographer"—monitoring, analyzing, and incorporating digital artifacts with the traditional ones. These include post-Soviet immigrant entrepreneurs' biographies available in open sources such as YouTube videos, personal and companies' websites, Russian-language media, including TV, online magazines, blogs, and social media profiles, and post-Soviet digital communities related to Austria, Spain, and Hungary.

The information about post-Soviet entrepreneurs is not always available as an open source. In these cases, information was collected through informal personal communication with representatives of the post-Soviet communities in these three countries and from Russian-language websites about Austria, Spain, and Hungary. In order to gather a representative sample of post-Soviet immigrant entrepreneurs in Austria, Spain, and Hungary, the author applied an innovative research method. This involved reviewing all EU-based Russian-language media and associations and thoroughly analyzing job vacancies and advertisements in them. For example, the most prominent and reliable source of information about post-Soviet immigrant entrepreneurs in Austria turned to be the *New Viennese Journal*, which served as the main source of information about these entrepreneurs. This was because most of them advertise their products and services in this long-standing Russian-language media in Austria. All issues of the *New Viennese Journal* from 2000 to 2020 were monitored, especially the rubric "Our Compatriots in Austria," where most interviews with entrepreneurs and hidden advertisements were published. Similarly, the author relied on the YouTube channel of the post-Soviet-owned company Alegria for information about post-Soviet immigrants in Spain and on the Russian-language journal *Russian Courier* and the website *Vengriya—Vzglyad Iznutri* (Hungary—The View from the Inside) for information about post-Soviet immigrant entrepreneurship in Hungary. The author's inquiry into post-Soviet immigrant entrepreneurship in Hungary was further complemented by observations from public and private Facebook groups, emails, telephone conversations, brief surveys based on initial findings, and participation in discussions.

The research resulted in a typology of post-Soviet immigrant entrepreneurship in terms of sectors and forms of businesses. The author had access to a group of post-Soviet Russian-speaking immigrants through some pre-existing personal contacts and Russian-language Facebook groups, majorly in Valencia and Alicante. She also met many post-Soviet immigrants, whose translation, construction, hospitality, and transfer services were used in the process of exploration. The author held both formal and informal conversations with them, establishing friendly relationships. From them the author learned details about their motives and experiences of immigration in Spain and paths to employment and entrepreneurship.

This was a convenience sample, which provided firm foundation for the study.

In the third phase of the study, the author conducted biographical interviews with at least one representative from each sector of post-Soviet immigrant entrepreneurship in Austria, Spain, and Hungary. The objective of these interviews was to verify the information collected through online sources through direct contact. The questionnaire included questions related to the motives behind emigration, immigration, and integration, as well as the reasons for becoming an entrepreneur and the financial sources used to start their enterprise. The following questions were included:

- What were/have been the channels of your integration?

When interviewing post-Soviet entrepreneurs, I also asked some of the following questions:

- What was the reason for becoming an entrepreneur?
- What were financial sources for starting your enterprise?
- What principles have you followed in choosing your business niche and partners?

The sample for these interviews consisted of post-Soviet immigrants across the three receiving countries, with roughly half of them being entrepreneurs or business owners that were met through professional or personal networks. Some of the participants were employees of local companies, multinational corporations (MNCs), or international organizations. In this stage of research, autoethnography served a major theory-building strategy in collecting data about post-Soviet immigrant entrepreneur's experiences across Europe. Adams et al. (2017) define autoethnography as a research approach that uses personal experiences to describe and interpret cultural texts, experiences, beliefs, and practices. Given its focus on personal experience, autoethnography also captures moments of everyday experience that cannot be captured through more traditional research methods. Using autoethnography as a fieldwork strategy allowed the researcher to incorporate what they saw, heard, and felt into the study. In this monograph, autoethnography was employed in two ways. First, the author, who is a close-to-native Russian speaker and has lived in Russia for almost two decades, drew upon her personal experiences as a migrant and the experiences of her acquaintances and friends who are post-Soviet immigrants. This immersion in these communities provided valuable insights into the experiences of post-Soviet immigrants in Austria, Spain, and Hungary. The author's continuous and frequent face-to-face and online conversations with these immigrants were recorded since 2013 in personal notes and served as a source of data for this book.

Secondly, the author is a member of many post-Soviet immigrant Facebook and Telegram public groups, such as "Ours in Austria," "Russians in Austria," "Russians in Spain," "Ukrainians in Spain," and "Russian-speaking Women in Hungary." By observing the content of discussions and participating in them, the author gained a systematic understanding of the thoughts and moods shared by these communities concerning their immigration and integration in host countries. When relevant, the results of surveys conducted within these digital communities were incorporated into this book as narratives reflecting their own interpretations of the role of entrepreneurship in integration. In Spain, the researcher gathered data on post-Soviet immigrants through Russian-speaking social networks and official associations of post-Soviet immigrants across Europe. This research stage involved over thirty informal semi-structured surveys and interviews (twenty face-to-face, five conducted online, and several conducted with associates of post-Soviet entrepreneurs when they were not available themselves) with post-Soviet immigrants who have lived in Spain for at least two years. The richest insights were obtained from life-story/biographical interviews with several post-Soviet immigrants, which provided a broader context for both immigration and entrepreneurship.

As a result, the number of interviewed post-Soviet immigrants and entrepreneurs residing in Austria, Spain, and Hungary reached a total of a hundred. Slightly less than two-thirds of them were female. All respondents were between the ages of twenty-eight and seventy, with the majority being between the ages of thirty and sixty. During this stage of research, the author encountered two obstacles. First, personal contacts with post-Soviet immigrants in all three countries were limited due to COVID-19 pandemic measures taken in all EU countries. This obstacle was overcome by conducting online interviews through different communication platforms, including telephone, WhatsApp, and Viber. Most of the interviews were recorded and then translated and transcribed verbatim. Others took the form of question-and-answer sessions via online messages.

The biographical data collected in this phase of research revealed that many post-Soviet entrepreneurs were cautious about openly discussing certain aspects of their businesses, particularly regarding financial sources used to establish them. As many social scientists who specialize on post-Soviet societies point out, these communities are suspicious, closed, and atomized due to being accustomed to the absence of strong formal institutions (Remennick, 2012; Rodgers et al., 2018). This trend was evident among the majority of post-Soviet immigrants, making it necessary for the author to have a level of embeddedness within these communities to access relevant information. To address these challenges, the following steps were taken: first, participants were recruited voluntarily; second, their names were replaced with descriptions of their roles; and third, the interview questions were carefully crafted in the final phase of research to minimize any discomfort and encourage open-ended responses. For instance: Have you utilized any grants or participated in any programs for start-ups or small businesses available in the host country?

Additionally, the author created anonymous online surveys and shared them in social media groups, clearly explaining the purpose and inviting willing participants. Guided by literature propositions, these questionnaires included open-ended questions with four to ten answer options, depending on the question: (a) What form(s) of economic activity or employment represents your primary source of income? (b) In which sector(s) of the economy do you work? (c) How would you describe your legal status? The questionnaires also captured demographic characteristics, such as age, gender, and year of immigration to the host country. As a result, the researcher received forty responses from across the EU.

Overall, out of the hundred interviews conducted, over thirty from each country, the fifty most representative ones were directly cited in this monograph. Similarly, out of the forty responses received through anonymous online surveys, the most significant parts of twenty of them were used. In the following text, the electronically recorded interviews and exact sentences recorded as the interviewee spoke are referred to as "personal communication." Similarly, all direct communication conducted online in the further text is referred as "online communication," while information obtained and cited from the social media groups in the text is referred as "social media group discussion," as summarized in Table 2.2.

All communication was conducted in Russian, then electronically systematized according to the answers and translated into English. There were also several cases of significant post-Soviet entrepreneurs, whose

Table 2.2 Methods of collection of the narratives referred in the text

Method of research	*Reference in the text*
Participant observation of post-Soviet immigrant communities, including face-to-face interviews, informal presence and conversations, and informal focus groups	Personal communication, a time when conducted
Interviews conducted via telephone, email, or online applications, and responses from surveys	Online communication, a time when conducted
Digital ethnography and virtual immigrant groups in social networks	Social media group discussion, a time when occurred

businesses were noteworthy, but who were not directly available for interviews. In these cases, when available, the author utilized interviews with these entrepreneurs published either by local Austrian, Spanish, and Hungarian media or by Russian-language media, either based in the EU or in some post-Soviet countries, discussing issues closely related to the research question addressed in this monograph. Used parts of these interviews were translated into English. When such information was not available, the researcher spoke to at least one knowledgeable acquaintance of these entrepreneurs and situated their narratives in the context of analysis. Finally, the collected data was systematized and analyzed within the theoretical framework developed in the previous chapter of this monograph in order to answer the research question. The focus of this study is on the thirty years following the collapse of the Soviet Union and the socialist bloc and the recent escalation of the war in Ukraine, which occurred on February 24, 2022, following Russia's full-fledged military invasion. During these three decades, the countries that were formerly part of the Soviet Union and constituted the Commonwealth of Independent States (CIS) have experienced multiple waves of emigration. The results of the investigation are presented in the three chapters that make up the second part of this monograph.

References

Adams, T., Ellis, C., & Holman Jones, S. (2017). Autoethnography. In *The International Encyclopedia of Communication Research Methods*. John Wiley & Sons, Inc.

Anderson, B. (1991). *Imagined Communities: Reflections on the Origin and Spread of Nationalism*. Verso.

Baubock, R. (2006). *Migration and Citizenship. Legal Status, Rights and Political Participation.*
Baycan, T., & Nijkamp, P. (2006). *Migrant Female Entrepreneurship—Driving Forces, Motivation and Performance* (2006-18).
Boettke, P., & Coyne, C. (2009). Context Matters: Institutions and Entrepreneur ship. *Foundations and Trends in Entrepreneurship, 5*, 135–209. https://doi.org/10.1561/0300000018
Boucher, A., & Gest, J. (2018). *Crossroads: Comparative Immigration Regimes in a World of Demographic Change*. Cambridge University Press.
Brubacker, R. (1992). *Citizenship and Nationhood in France and Germany*. Harvard University Press.
Caliandro, A. (2014). *The Difference between Netnography and Digital Ethnography.*
Castles, S. (1995). How Nation-States Respond to Immigration and Ethnic Diversity. *Journal of Ethnic and Migration Studies, 21*(3), 293–308.
European Parliament. (2016). Regulation (EU) 2016/399 of the European Parliament and of the Council of 9 March 2016 on a Union Code on the Rules Governing the Movement of Persons Across Borders (Schengen Borders Code).
Halse, L. (2022). What's an Immigration Regime? Exploring Migration Patterns Worldwide.
Heleniak, T. (2017). Post-Soviet Russian-Speaking Migration to the UK: The Discourses of Visibility and Accountability. In *Post-Soviet Migration and Diasporas: From Global Perspectives to Everyday Practices*. Palgrave Pivot.
Kovacevic-Bielicki, D., & Pejovic, A. (2020). *Extreme Digital Push in a World Changed by COVID-19: Experiences and Reflections on Doing Social Research Online.*
Kozinets, R. (2015). *Netnography. Doing Ethnographic Research Online*. SAGE.
Miller, D. (2018). *Digital Anthropology. Cambridge Encyclopedia of Anthropology.*
Pink, S., Horst, H., Postill, J., Hjorth, L., Lewis, T., & Tacchi, J. (2016). *Digital Ethnography: Principles and Practice*. Sage Publications.
Polanyi, K. (1944). *The Great Transformation: The Political and Economic Origins of Our Time*. Beacon Press.
Remennick, L. (2012). *Russian Jews on Three Continents. Identity, Integration, and Conflict*. Transaction Publisher.
Rodgers, P., Vershanina, N., Williams, C., & Theodorakopoulos, N. (2018). Leveraging Symbolic Capital: The Use of Blat Networks Across Transnational Spaces. *Global Networks, 19*(1), 119–136.
Ryazantsev, S., Pismennaya, E., Lukyantsev, A., Sivoplyasova, S., & Khramova, M. (2018). Modern Emigration from Russia and Formation of Russian-Speaking Communities Abroad (In Russian). *World Economy and International Relations, 62*(6), 93–107.
Skageby, J. (2011). Online Ethnographic Methods: Towards a Qualitative Understanding of Virtual Community Practices. In *Handbook of Research on*

Methods and Techniques for Studying Virtual Communities: Paradigms and Phenomena (pp. 410–428). IGI Global.

Statistics Austria—Migration. (2021–2022). https://www.statistik.at/en/statistics/population-and-society/population/migration-and-naturalisation/migration-total

Tepavcevic, S. (2017). Immigrant Entrepreneurship in the Post-Socialist Countries of the European Union: Motives and Patterns of Entrepreneurship of Post-Soviet Immigrants in Hungary. *Migration and Ethnic Themes, 1*, 65–92.

Tepavcevic, S. (2020). *Homo Sovieticus or the Agent of Change?*

Tepavcevic, S. (2021). Changing Geography, Retaining the Mentality: Social and Economic Integration of Post-Soviet Immigrants in Austria and Hungary. *Review of Economic Theory and Policy, 3*, 137–154.

Tepavcevic, S., Molodikova, I., & Ryazantsev, S. (2020). Post-Soviet Russian-Language Migration, Investment, and Entrepreneurship in Eastern and Central Europe (for Example of Hungary, Austria, and the Czech Republic). *Today and Tomorrow of the Russian Economy [In Russian], 99–100*, 5–22.

Weinar, A. (2018). Politics of Emigration in Europe. In *The Routledge Handbook of the Politics of Migration in Europe* (pp. 62–73). Routledge.

Wesch, M. (2009). YouTube and You: Experiences of Self-awareness in the Context Collapse of the Recording Webcam. *Explorations in Media Ecology, 8*(2), 19–34.

Zimmerman, K. F. (2005). *European Migration. What Do We Know?* Oxford University Press.

PART II

CHAPTER 3

Post-Soviet Entrepreneurship in Coordinated Variety of Market Economy: The Case of Austria

Abstract This chapter delves into the examination of the impact of entrepreneurship on the integration of post-Soviet immigrants in Austria, which is classified as a coordinated market economy (CME) by the Varieties of Capitalism (VoC) framework. Despite Austria's attraction as a destination for immigrants due to its high standard of living, social protection, soft climate, and rich cultural heritage, post-Soviet immigrants face limited access to the labor market and limited opportunities for entrepreneurship. As a result, post-Soviet immigrant entrepreneurs tend to establish more partnerships with other immigrants than with indigenous Austrians. The chapter reveals and categorizes the three forms of post-Soviet entrepreneurship in Austria based on their position in the Austrian market, their relationship with the post-Soviet immigrant community, and their contribution to integration.

Keywords Capitalism variety • Coordinate market • Austria • Immigration regime • Immigrant entrepreneurship • Immigrants' integration

S. Tepavcevic, *Diversity of Migrant Entrepreneurship in Varieties of European Capitalism*,
https://doi.org/10.1007/978-3-031-31097-3_3

3.1 Introduction: Austria's Economic Model and Immigration

Austria's transition to a military-neutral country followed the withdrawal of the Soviet Army in 1955. Vienna, the Austrian capital, emerged as the hub for many international organizations, including the International Atomic Energy Agency (IEA), the Organization of Petroleum Exporting Countries (OPEC), and the Organization for Security and Cooperation in Europe (OSCE). The presence of these organizations in Vienna attracted a diverse group of international employees. At the same time, the Austrian political grand coalition's post-war economic policy guided by the Keynesian philosophy and aimed at full employment was supported by high government spending. In the late 1950s and in the 1960s, Austria saw rapid economic growth, with its GDP increasing by over 6 percent annually. The rapidly expanding industries required a larger workforce than what was available among the Austrians, leading employers to demand foreign labor (Kraler, 2011). At the same time, workers' unions resisted the employment of foreign citizens to prevent wage suppression for the local workforce. These tensions and the efforts to balance conflicting interests resulted in the formation of the Austrian economic model, which relied on a system of coordination and cooperation between various market and non-market actors, including a salary range system based on qualifications.

In the mid-1970s, Austria experienced a slowdown in economic growth like many other countries due to the oil crisis. However, Austria has maintained its status as one of the top twenty world economies since the 1990s according to World Bank data ("World Bank National Accounts Data, Austria GDP growth," 2022). In 1995, Austria joined the EU along with Finland and Sweden. The country has a relatively high real GDP per capita (measuring the total economic output of a country divided by the number of people and adjusted for inflation) and a relatively low Gini Coefficient (that measures wealth equality), indicating a prosperous economy with relatively equal wealth distribution (Table 3.1).

Austria has become a significant destination for immigrants as it has developed economically (Van Mol & de Valk, 2016). By 2019, people with immigrant background made up more than 16 percent of Austria's population (Austria Government, 2019). Although Austria was a major target country during the 2015 migration crisis, it has low levels of entrepreneurship, as indicated by the Global Entrepreneurship Monitor (GEM)

Table 3.1 Austria—real GDP per capita and Gini Coefficient in selected years

Year	*2010*	*2015*	*2020*
Real GDP per capita in Euro per capita	35.398	36.148	35.480
Gini Coefficient (0 = total equality, 1 = total inequality)	28.3	27.2	27.8

Source: "Eurostat, 2022 Real GDP per capita," (2022)

(2021). Despite its good economic performance and attraction to immigrants, the institutional framework of a CME in Austria, as classified by the VoC, is characterized by multilevel coordination between market and non-market actors, such as firms and workers unions, cooperation between firms rather than competition, and a relatively high level of social equality.

The goal of this chapter is to examine the ways in which coordination between market and non-market actors in a CME like Austria affects immigrant entrepreneurship. Through analyzing the emergence and development of post-Soviet communities in Austria, the chapter explores the impact of the country's immigration regime on immigrant entrepreneurship. Most businesses established and run by post-Soviet immigrants in Austria, such as those in social services, education, construction, logistics, and media cater primarily to Russian-speaking communities or international customers, with the exception of a few sectors like private medical services, real estate, construction, and retail, which also serve Austrian customers. The chapter also analyzes the changes in the Austrian immigration regime and the functioning of post-Soviet immigrant communities in Austria. The classification of post-Soviet immigrant entrepreneurship in Austria based on the criteria described in Chap. 2 is also presented. Finally, the role of entrepreneurship in the integration of post-Soviet immigrants in Austria is discussed and the findings are placed within the context of existing theories of entrepreneurship in CMEs and immigrant entrepreneurship.

3.2 The Dynamics of Austrian Immigration Regime: "Integration Before New Immigration"

Austria's immigration regime has a long history, beginning with the restrictive Protection of Native Workers Act in 1925. During World War II and the decade that followed, increasing numbers of refugees from neighboring countries arrived in Austria, including Germans who settled and received citizenship as *jus sanguine*. However, during the Soviet military interventions in Hungary in 1956 and Czechoslovakia in 1968, most refugees—180,000 from Hungary and 162,000 from Czechoslovakia—who fled to Austria continued their journey to the USA and Western Europe. Despite this, the shortage of labor in the local industries in the late 1950s, due to the rapid growth of the Austrian economy, led to the establishment of bilateral agreements in 1961 for the temporary employment of foreign labor force from Southern European countries and Turkey, following negotiations between employers and trade unions (Kraler, 2011) (Table 3.2).

The fall of the socialist bloc and the collapse of several communist regimes in Eastern and Southern Europe in the early 1990s brought a new wave of migrants to Austria, causing the migration policy to become politicized. This led to the creation of the Residence Act, the first regulation that recognized the need for immigrant integration. Austria's accession to the EEA in 1994 and the EU in 1995 hastened the harmonization of Austria's immigration regime within the EU's. In 2010, Austria adopted a neoliberal, Canada-style immigration policy, proposed by the Austrian Association of Industrialists, to attract more highly skilled immigrants. The association also created a platform of companies supporting integration measures (Perchinig, 2013). However, Huddleston et al. (2011) argued that Austria's integration policy is still restrictive compared with other EU countries, with weak commitments to targeted labor market measures and migrants' political participation, and some of the most restrictive conditions for family reunification in Europe. Kraler (2011, p. 48) noted that despite this, "[T]he reality at the local level has always been quite different, seeing various forms emerge for the pragmatic accommodation of immigrants' needs." To summarize, Austria's immigration regime has evolved from a highly restrictive *jus sanguinis*, typical of CMEs, to a highly restrictive *jus soli*. The accuracy of immigrant data in Austria is uncertain due to the collection of most socioeconomic data being based on citizenship, which excludes naturalized immigrants. The naturalization process in Austria is highly selective in socioeconomic status, favoring wealthier immigrants. However, data from the GEM (Global Entrepreneurship Monitor, 2021) shows that around 9 percent of the Austrian population are entrepreneurs, while Austria's data on migration (Austria Government, 2019) shows that around 20 percent of the population are immigrants. This suggests that entrepreneurship might play a role in the integration of some immigrants in Austria. The well-regulated labor

Table 3.2 Evolvement of Austria's immigration regime

Significant regulation/year	*Aim*	*Outcome*
Protection of Native Workers Act (Inlandarbeiterschutzgesetz) 1925	The act established a system of work permits for foreign citizens	The act shifted control from the public welfare system to labor market and its authorities, increasing the role of the state in the regulation of employment
Bilateral Agreements with Spain—1961; Yugoslavia and Turkey—1966	An expression of the expansion of neocorporatist modes of welfare and labor market policymaking based on the idea that labor markets had a limited "absorption capacity" (Kraler, 2011, p. 28)	Partial state's control of labor market
Asylum act 1968	Accommodation of Czechoslovak refugees	Self-perception of a "safe haven" for refugees; Czechoslovaks, who escaped from the Soviet invasion.
Act of Employment of Foreign Workers (Ausländerbeschäftigungsgesetz) 1975	From then on, employers had to prove they could not fill vacancies with equally qualified nationals before an employment permit was issued (Kraler, 2011, p. 30)	legalized informal quota system; entrenched employers' dominant position in relation to migrants'; prioritized nationals over foreigners on the labor market
Residence Act 1992	The first regulation to recognize the need of integration of immigrants	Regulation related to the time of immigration and the German language knowledge—these became important factors in integration of immigrants

(*continued*)

Table 3.2 (continued)

Significant regulation/year	*Aim*	*Outcome*
A formal citizenship test was introduced and the Common European Framework of Reference for Languages's (CEFRL) A2—2006	Modeled after the Netherlands' and Germany's local language knowledge policies	An ethnicity-based model of citizenship—first and foremost granted to people with Austrian parents (Baubock, 2006); naturalization is one of the riskiest and most expensive gambles in [the] EU (Huddleston et al. (2011, p. 27))
National Plan for Integration (NAPI)—2009	The need to provide opportunities for migrants and to counter discrimination and xenophobia	The obligations of migrants, rather than those of the state or the public (Kraler, 2011)
The language level increased further to CEFRL B1—2011		Applicants need to document for the last three years a minimum income and funds for rent, loan repayment, garnishments, and alimony

Source: Baubock (2006); Kraler (2011); Huddleston et al. (2011)

market and trustworthy legal system in Austria are attractive to migrants, enhancing the establishment of small-scale and low-tech businesses by immigrants. High-tech manufacturing and innovation, on the other hand, tend to be dominated by large Austrian companies and multinational corporations. The following sections examine the validity of these assumptions regarding post-Soviet immigrant communities in Austria.

3.3 Post-Soviet Immigrant Communities in Austria: Waves and Modes of Immigration

Post-Soviet immigration to Austria is comprised of five distinct waves. The first was relatively small and consisted of Soviet representatives in international organizations in Vienna and post-Soviet Jews who immigrated to

Austria in the late 1980s. The second wave was largely made up of around 22,000 Chechen refugees who either arrived as asylum-seekers in the early 1990s with Soviet passports or illegally, making them underrepresented in official Austrian statistics (Molodikova, 2019). The existing studies suggest that the representatives of this wave of post-Soviet immigration in Austria remain socially unsettled because of

> an unwritten list of 'honorable' (permissible) male (masculine) types of jobs, such as a trainer in a sport club, a guard in a security firm, a driver or a builder, but not a servant or a cleaner. The constrains to the legal economic activity are complicated due to the lack of language skills and low qualifications of the first generation of Chechen migrants. (Molodikova, 2019, p. 124)

Facing the disparity between cultural customs, the need to support their families, and the demands of the local labor market, certain individuals within this immigration wave have become involved in various criminal activities. These activities include human trafficking across EU borders and engaging in rent-seeking practices by extorting protection fees from other immigrants (Szczepanikova, 2008).

The third wave consisted mostly of post-Soviet students who arrived in Austria in the late 1990s, as well as descendants of Austrian soldiers who were held as hostages in Russia during World War I and immediately received Austrian citizenship (personal communication, October 2021). This group came from various former Soviet republics, primarily speaking Russian, and it is difficult to determine their size as many have become Austrian citizens and entrepreneurs over the last two decades. Depending on the type of activity, they all function as either small businesses, individual entrepreneurs, or non-governmental organizations. The fourth wave took place between 2000 and 2013 and was primarily made up of post-Soviet business and political elites, investing primarily in real estate, hospitality, and manufacturing. The fifth and most recent wave arrived from Russia and Ukraine since 2014, largely due to the conflict in Ukraine and the related crisis, and was mostly made up of middle-class Russians and Ukrainians. As of January 1, 2022, the estimated number of post-Soviet immigrants in Austria was 46,000, including approximately 34,000 Russians and close to 13,000 Ukrainians ("Statistics Austria—migration," 2021–2022). Many relatively young post-Soviet immigrants in Austria until 2022 worked for large Austrian and Russia-based transnational corporations, with significant representations in Austria, such as GazpromNeft,

Sberbank, Sibur, VTB, and Lukoil (Tepavcevic, 2018). They used their bilingual skills in Russian and German and Austrian higher education certificates to secure employment in these companies, providing them access to the Austrian labor market (personal communication, October 2021).

The post-Soviet communities in Austria are among the smaller immigrant groups, with former Yugoslav and Turkish communities being the largest. Despite their size, they are well-connected and present in nearly all parts of Austria. To connect with one another, they utilize social media platforms such as Facebook and also have virtual meeting points like the *New Viennese Journal* or the Russian Austrian website. These platforms often serve as both ethnic businesses and points of connection for the post-Soviet immigrant communities. The existence of these communities highlights a trend among post-Soviet emigrants who have tended to move to countries with advanced market economies and substantial financial resources in the late 1990s and beyond. In Austria, post-Soviet immigrants have founded several associations across cities such as Vienna, Graz, Linz, and Salzburg. These associations serve either to support life and integration in the cities where they have settled, like "Russian speakers in Linz" (personal communication, October 2021), or to support professional interests, like the "Association of Teachers" (personal communication, October 2021). The reasons for immigration to Austria vary among individuals. Some Soviet couples immigrated to Vienna before the collapse of the USSR in 1987 due to one of spouses' job with an international organization (online communication, May 2020). Others from the Former Soviet Union (FSU) immigrated via other countries.

> I was born in Dushanbe, I lived there for seventeen years ... Then we moved to Israel. We spent there seven years. After these seven years in Israel we moved further to Vienna, because we had a lot of relatives here. At the same time, the climate, friends, relatives—everything was much closer to us here in Austria. (Online communication, March 2020)

On the one hand, the collapse of the USSR and the related crisis prevented Soviet citizens who have already moved to Austria from considering the option of returning to their home countries. On the other hand, it generated the first massive immigration wave from the former Soviet republics to Austria during the 1990s. Post-Soviet immigrants in Austria extensively used free higher education as an opportunity to study and stay in Austria. As owner of a small real estate maintenance company explained,

"[F]irst I came as tourist, and then I passed the exam to the institute of music as a student of music" (online communication, February 2020). The co-owner of the attorney-at-law office initially came to Austria to study and then stayed to work. "The path of becoming a lawyer is very long: one has to do the internship in a court for a very small salary, then one has to work as an assistant to a lawyer—overall this practice before the exam to become a lawyer takes five years" (personal communication, February 2020).

A significant number of real estate purchases, including hotels in central Vienna, characterized the immigration of post-Soviet business and political elites to Austria between 2000 and 2013. The most striking example was the family of the late former Moscow mayor, Yuriy Luzhkov: his spouse and the richest Russian woman in the 2000s, Elena Baturina purchased significant number of various real estate properties across Austria, including some hotels in the center of Vienna (Bikova, 2011). A migration consultant noted that 55 percent of those seeking their services aimed to establish or operate businesses in Austria while continuing to live and work in Russia, while only 36 percent sought to move their families to Austria and only 9 percent intended to permanently relocate ("'Pravda' program," 2016). This suggests that for many post-Soviet immigrants, Austria served as an "additional airport" rather than a permanent residence. In addition, half of the respondents came to Austria as marriage immigrants. One of them, the owner of one of the Russian schools, simply explained, "I did not plan to move to Austria, but since I met my wonderful husband, the decision to move was automatic" (online communication, March 2020).

In contrast to the propositions made by Rath (2006) and Waldinger (2009), who argue that better living standards and investment opportunities are the primary motivations for migration, the search for stability and security is a key driver for post-Soviet immigration to Austria. This is especially true for those who arrived in Austria after the conflict in Ukraine began in 2014. As one post-Soviet immigrant who works for an Austrian real estate company stated, "We moved to Austria in 2014 for security reasons. Russian security structures started prosecution against my husband with the goal of taking over his business in the coal industry. He said that the children and I had to leave the country. My friend lived in Austria and ensured me that it was safe and quiet here. Her lawyer helped me find a job here, and I moved to work in Austria, taking the children with me" (online communication, March 2020). Similarly, one well-known Russian entrepreneur and former politician relocated to Austria to avoid political prosecution for his financial support of the non-systemic opposition. In an interview with Russian independent media TVRain (2019), he stated that the political and economic risks in Russia were significantly higher than in Austria. This challenges the notion that post-Soviet immigration to Austria is solely motivated by a desire for better living standards and investment opportunities. In sum, the reasons for immigration from the former Soviet Union to Austria appear to be more complex, including factors such as marriage, family reunification, seeking safety, and avoiding political and economic persecution. These findings further solidify Austria's reputation as a country with a stable political and economic system.

3.4 Classification of Post-Soviet Immigrant Entrepreneurship in Austria

As noted in Chap. 2, the criteria for classification of post-Soviet entrepreneurship consists of three factors: the place in host country's market reflected in the size and sector of entrepreneurship, the relation of entrepreneurship to the post-Soviet immigrant community, and the role of entrepreneurship in immigrants' integration in a host country. According to personal communication conducted between February 2020 and November 2021, many post-Soviet immigrants to Austria initially had the ambition to open restaurants targeting wealthy customers. However, the lack of demand resulted in the quick closure of these establishments. For instance, the restaurant Moskva, located in the center of Vienna, which opened in the early 2000s, faced a similar fate to the restaurant Vladimir, named after another Russian city: both closed in less than a decade. These examples highlight the complexity of migration motives, which can involve a combination of necessity and opportunity factors. This is further emphasized in an interview that showcases the nuanced nature of entrepreneurship motivations.

> I worked in the music school. There the working hours start at 2 p.m. and I worked usually until 9 p.m. When my daughter was born, this became very inconvenient, because kindergartens start to work at 7 a.m. and work until 4–5 p.m. ... When I realized that I have to change something, another opportunity emerged. My former student ... founded architecture-real estate bureau, and I told him that I plan to find a part-time work in order to

spend more time with my daughter. … He offered me to work part-time in his company. I started there from accounting, in parallel I took and finished accountancy courses, and then he saw that I am a good learner, and he offered me to choose to do what I am interested. I chose real-estate management and agency courses. … I wanted to continue. Unfortunately, the company lost its major client, and I started to look for something that I can do independently in that sector, so I founded my own company. (Online communication, February 2020)

Therefore, female migrant entrepreneurship became the solution to the lifestyle changes brought on by childcare responsibilities and job loss due to bankruptcy (personal communication, February 2020). The former was the catalyst for a career shift and presented an opportunity, while the latter seemed to be more of a short-term necessity and a search for long-term prospects. Another post-Soviet entrepreneur initially received an immigration permit and built his career as an employee at an Austrian company. He then used that experience as a stepping-stone to establish a family-run business independently.

When I started to work at the shop, my boss hired a good lawyer, who made all the paperwork for me. I received visa in one month, while usually that process takes six months. … My younger brother also worked with me. After six years of working in that company, my brother and I decided to open our own jewelry shop. (Online communication March 2020)

For some post-Soviet immigrants in Austria, the main motivation for starting their own business was to utilize their education and skills. They believed the best way to do this was by establishing a language and arts school.

I have been educated for several different professions on different levels, including classic musicology, and pedagogy, the latter is my main profession. I am not the first generation of pedagogues in my family, I have been working in that sphere for a long time and I am very interested in pedagogy. … The School is how I see myself in the current moment. To me it is …an international and interdisciplinary approach to the education. I think that one does not need to be a politician to unite people … to me it is important to provide them with live and interesting education. (Online communication, March 2020)

Thus, in this particular case of post-Soviet entrepreneurship in Austria, both immigration and entrepreneurship were motivated by opportunities. Finally, for one respondent, entrepreneurship was a means of escaping poverty experienced in childhood. Interestingly, this ambition driven by trauma was shared with their German husband.

> Both of us, when we were kids, made a promise to ourselves that we will never be as poor as our parents. …It is rather your childhood promise to yourself that you will live better than your parents do. You will have everything that you want … For all of entrepreneurs that I have ever met… the main motive has been the fact that they grew up without money. (Personal communication, February 2020)

Another entrepreneur from Kazakhstan confirms this view by comparing the ambitions of post-Soviet immigrants in Austria with the local population. According to her statement in an online communication in February 2020, "Austrians are 'full', they feel satisfied, and they feel convenient. Convenience is the most important for them. Our people are hungry, and they have goals to fulfil, so they are motivated." This highlights that the motives for entrepreneurship are usually a combination of necessities and opportunities, ranging from building a self-sustainable family business, earning more than a typical employee salary, making a better work-life balance, and overcoming poverty-related traumas from childhood. Additionally, these statements emphasize that the motives for entrepreneurship among post-Soviet immigrant entrepreneurs in Austria are rarely, if at all, related to the immigration process.

The example of Luxury Immobilien, a real estate developer company owned by post-Soviet Russian-speaking entrepreneurs and belonging to the Metropolitan Group with headquarters in Dubai, reveals how some of these entrepreneurs in Austria focus on opportunities in the economically advanced market. As the company's description on its website suggests, Luxury Immobilien specializes in the development and trade of luxury real estate and is oriented toward wealthy third-country nationals (TCNs). The company offers a full range of services in the Austrian real estate market, including buying, selling, and renting residential and commercial properties, as well as obtaining a residence permit in Austria and financing options for property purchases. Additionally, they offer interior design, consultation, and legal support from their highly skilled lawyers (2022).

Similarly, the theater company *Russkaya Gostinaya* (the Russian Guestroom), which operated between 2016 and 2021 and organized performances of famous Russian theaters (2016) in Vienna for relatively wealthy post-Soviet immigrants in Austria, constitutes an example of connector-type immigrant entrepreneurship, characterized by its sector, size, and role in the immigrant community and social integration of its founder. Similar to culture-related Russian immigrant entrepreneurship that Byford (2012) explored in the UK, organizing performances in Vienna, the Russian Guestroom cooperated with the Russian House (the Russian cultural center in Vienna). However, its owner reported that the interest was not as high as expected and the COVID-19 lockdowns worsened the chances of further developing the project, leading to its temporary halt, despite its website still being active (personal communication, October 2021).

In contrast to the theater company, the post-Soviet-owned educational centers continue to flourish in Austria, particularly in Vienna. While some of these centers specialize in music and art classes, such as *Garmonia* (Harmony), others, such as *Meridian*, focus on the Russian language and literature. There are also post-Soviet founded schools that offer a combination of classes in music, arts, and both Russian and German languages, such as *Perfekt*. Located in downtown Vienna, *Perfekt* provides student-tailored classes in arts and languages and caters to a mostly immigrant and Austrian-post-Soviet origin customer base (personal communication, October 2021). Despite the traditional coordination between companies working in the same sector in Austria, these post-Soviet immigrant-founded schools display high levels of competition both for qualified employees and for customers (personal interview, February 2020). The motives for entrepreneurship among these schools also appear to vary, with some driven primarily by profits while others prioritize the application of their founders' knowledge and pedagogical skills (personal communication, October 2021).

The analysis of post-Soviet immigrant entrepreneurship in social and mass media reveals a significant number of self-employed entrepreneurs or micro-companies providing services in various industries, including beauty, logistics, construction, and tourism. Due to their low-scale services and production and targeting mostly their former compatriots, along with advertising their services in relevant media and social media groups, these businesses represent the same type of immigrant entrepreneurship. Given their small size and focus on serving the immigrant community, this type of immigrant entrepreneurship can be classified as grassroots entrepreneurship.

Similarly, the growth of post-Soviet immigrant communities in Austria has led to the creation of several Russian-language media outlets. Some of these, such as the *New Viennese Journal*, have been operating for over two decades and serve as small culture-based businesses. The journal, which is both online and offline, covers cultural, political, and business topics and is partially run by an informal leader of the post-Soviet community in Austria, who coordinates with pan-European associations of Russian compatriots (personal communication, October, 2021). *Russian Austria* is another informational news portal that also serves as an online forum for Russian-speaking immigrants in Austria.

There are also several YouTube channels and web portals devoted to the post-Soviet immigrant communities in Austria and the EU such as "Expat Life," "Focus-Austria," and "Emigrant Guru." These outlets provide news and analytical content, as well as migration consultancy, and generate revenue from both advertisement and subscription-based services. They cater primarily to a relatively large number of self-employed individuals, who provide medical, legal, and other social services in both German and Russian languages. The presence of these media outlets in Austria supports the theory of demand and supply in ethnic, common culture-based enclaves. Their size, sector, role in the post-Soviet community in Austria, and their economic integration make these entrepreneurs and their activities important connectors between members of the post-Soviet community in Austria, constituting a separate type of immigrant entrepreneurship, referred to as "connector immigrant entrepreneurship."

The formation of a cultural enclave market among post-Soviet immigrants in Austria can be attributed to the challenges they face during the immigration and integration process, as well as in starting a business. Interviews with these immigrants revealed that regardless of their initial motivations for immigration, they all encountered bureaucratic hurdles in obtaining immigration documents, such as visas, work permits, or citizenship. These difficulties have contributed to the formation of a market that serves the specific needs and interests of the post-Soviet community in Austria. Further research is needed to fully understand the impact of these challenges on the formation and development of immigrant entrepreneurship in Austria.

> The only aspect that affects each immigrant here is the visa issue, through which each migrant has to go through each year. It is especially hard to go through it in migration offices here, in Vienna... If you have all the documents needed, you might be ok. They are very strict on checking each of your steps: where have you been? what did you do. (Online communication, February 2020)

Despite the entry into force of the Schengen Agreement and the equal application of immigration procedures to all TCNs in the EU, many of the post-Soviet immigrants interviewed had already been residing in Austria either prior to its EU membership or prior to 2008. This has resulted in limited access to the Austrian labor market for TCNs, a factor cited by all respondents as a significant challenge in their integration process in Austria. "Austrians have very strong protection of their labor market. Thus, the Austrians and the EU citizens are the priority. Specialists from third countries are secondary choice" (online communication, February 2020). Apart from the legal sphere, some entrepreneurs experienced indirect gender-based professional discrimination.

> I opened the attorney-at-law office myself alone, and my business started well off. Soon, I understood that my independent work is perceived by some people as a negative aspect: if I work alone for large projects—that is first reason; the second aspect is that I am a woman and it is not perceived seriously in this type of job among Austrians. ... Austrians are very conservative, if compared to Russians and Ukrainians. It is still widely regarded that a male lawyer is better than a female lawyer is. ...I have heard such a comment many times. Therefore, for me it was important that one of my partners is a male. Once he comes with me to the meeting, they perceive me better, more seriously. In my view, this stereotype among Austrians is still quite present. (Personal communication, February 2020)

Furthermore, other post-Soviet female entrepreneurs seem to experience a type of alienation from Austrians, based on their foreign status, rather than their gender.

> The Austrian society is highly sterile, highly class-based. ... [t]here are divisions between the people on "ours" and "others". ...it turns out, that if you

haven't go here to the kindergarten, school, or in the university, chances to be accepted into various social groups are very low, except if you integrate with other expats, who, like myself, moved here relatively recently. (Personal communication, February 2020)

Thus, while some post-Soviet immigrant entrepreneurs in Austria have encountered various forms of indirect social discrimination, they all faced legal obstacles during the integration process. Those who immigrated more recently encountered greater challenges in both social and legal integration, which they attempted to address by networking and engaging with post-Soviet immigrant associations in Austria.

I became a member of a creative organization "*Bereginya*," Russian-speaking female society (founded to help) in integration in Austria ... everyone works on voluntary basis. That helps me to build the networks to gain more pupils for my classes, as that is the best advertisement... For each event they prepare video, photos, recommendations, and it creates the portfolio... people start to recognize me and then they contact me to provide private classes for their kids. Then I provide private Russian language classes, and actor-master-classes at home. (Personal communication, February 2020)

Furthermore, while being female in certain professions may present a challenge in the Austrian market, this can be seen as an advantage in the post-Soviet cultural enclave market. Conversely, an immigrant background can be perceived as a comparative advantage for post-Soviet entrepreneurs in the Austrian market.

Most of my clients—95 percent—are men; they are men from the former Soviet Union. ... They are raised in a very different way than Austrians, in the society and ideology where everyone were equal. As a result, absolute majorities of successful men from the FSU consider that women better do this type of work that I do, because women are more accurate and they make less mistakes, and they are more patient. ... If I did not have the knowledge of the Russian language, my career as an independent lawyer would be much harder, because there are so many lawyers. For me an assistant, who does not speak Russian, is useless. In the reality, there is an equal need in very good, grammatically correct with no accent knowledge of German and Russian languages. (Personal communication, February 2020)

This experience aligns with the findings of Light (1984) and Portes (1997) that immigrants use the demand from their ethnic communities to cater to their needs. It also supports the argument of Dunnecker and Cakir (2016) that geographic mobility and proficiency in multiple languages are important qualities for female immigrant entrepreneurs. Furthermore, the post-Soviet entrepreneurship in Austria demonstrates that, despite their small size, many of these businesses have been operating for over a decade. An example of this is the *New Viennese Journal*, which relies on advertisement revenue, while the journal's owner diversifies her business by offering also a range of immigration services. However, the longevity of another post-Soviet immigrant's jewelry business, established over three decades ago, highlights the importance of personal qualities and independence from the cultural enclave ("New Viennese Journal," 2020).

> There are tourists, of course, but the majority are the locals ... I have never made a choice of employees based on their origin. I had a good friend of mine from Syria, who worked with me. Now I have an employee from Poland, I also work closely with Austrians, and with one Australian, so to me it is not a problem. ... Even most important is that it is a good person, and then a good professional. Because one can become a good professional, but it is hard to learn to be a good person. (Online communication, March 2020)

Therefore, the businesses established by Soviet citizens in Austria in the late 1980s form part of and operate within the cultural enclave market, which coincides with the findings of Shvarts (2010) in Canada. Both the owner of a real estate agency and the owner of a jewelry shop reported similar experiences regarding their main customers.

> All my clients are Austrians, German-speakers, because my clients are directed from my main job... This work created me such a possibility to offer certain services to my clients. They—the company where I worked—were dealing only with property management, while clients want to sell and buy and rent their property. Therefore, I offer them my services in real estate trade. (Online communication, February 2020)

Other experiences of post-Soviet entrepreneurs in Austria show not only a high degree of integration into the Austrian mainstream market but also a trend of supplementing their entrepreneurship with part-time employment in larger companies to increase their income. This is confirmed by the testimony of several post-Soviet immigrant entrepreneurs, indicating that this is becoming a more common practice.

> I have an official contract with the agency that offers apartments for tourists on short-term basis. That is my part-time job, 16 hours a week… the owners are Russians… it provides a stable income. … I have the movie about the musician that I am finishing now; then I have my authorized trainings that I provide as a member of the social organization, then I provide private lessons for kids at home, and I work as a manager at the tourist company. (Personal communication. February 2020)

This example offers insight into three theories related to immigrant entrepreneurship. Firstly, the necessity thesis, which suggests that immigrants become entrepreneurs due to a lack of employment opportunities in the host country or the presence of opportunities in the host country or the presence of opportunities in cultural enclave markets, is partially challenged by this finding. The example shows that immigrants also become entrepreneurs because of their willingness to provide more flexible services than locals. Secondly, the opportunity thesis is extended by demonstrating that, in addition to cultural enclave markets, immigrant entrepreneurship can also be based on opportunities in the mainstream market of the host country and part-time employment in local companies, as evidenced by the example of the small real estate agency owner.

Furthermore, this example highlights the positive impact of even part-time access to the host country's labor market for immigrants, not only benefiting locals through the provision of services but also strengthening the coordinative model of the Austrian market and its focus on social protection. As a result, this type of immigrant business acts as a connector within the immigrant community and generates a "connectors" type of immigrant entrepreneurship. Similarly, this example also highlights the presence of both small and large post-Soviet immigrant businesses in Austria and their challenges and solutions. The experience of a large hospitality business, owned by a famous Russian businessperson, demonstrates the challenges faced by post-Soviet entrepreneurs in Austria, such as the lack of reliable labor force and the long-term returns on investments. To overcome this challenge, the business owner employed workers from Central and Eastern EU member states and provided services to both local and international clients, thus operating as a part of the Austrian mainstream market (TVRain, 2019). This can be conceptualized as the investment-based corporation-like type of immigrant business. The post-Soviet owner of a Vienna-based attorney-at-law office confirms a similar trend among other relatively large businesses conducted by post-Soviet entrepreneurs in Austria. This supports the theory of investment-based immigrant entrepreneurship and highlights the importance of the coordination of local market and non-market actors in Austria in determining the success of immigrant businesses.

> These businesses are very different, but they are not oriented only to Russian speakers. These are companies from hard industries, chemical industry, textile industry, jewelry industry ... Given the political and legal situation in Ukraine and Russia, many are concerned that their businesses can be taken over there, so they decide to operate their businesses through Austrian companies. ... Majority of the businesses operate in the countries of the former Soviet Union. (Personal communication, February 2020)

The large post-Soviet businesses that have relocated to Austria while continuing to operate in their home countries provide evidence of the transnationalism theory in immigrant entrepreneurship literature (Ren & Liu, 2015). This theory postulates that migrant entrepreneurs are increasingly operating their businesses in both the host and home countries. Additionally, some small businesses established by more recent post-Soviet immigrants in Austria are internet-based and operate as part of transnational and global markets (Ren & Liu, 2015).

> I am a transnational entrepreneur, but it is only because the IT is such a sector.... I have a customer in Poland, I work in Austria, and I have the candidates from all over the world: Canada, USA, Philippines ...Different companies require different human resources; therefore, the geography of my work is global. (Personal communication, February 2020)

Despite the type of businesses that they operate and generally positive impressions regarding the socio-political system in Austria, most post-Soviet immigrant entrepreneurs in Austria have similar impressions about the significant level of their exclusion from the Austrian market and society directly related to its economic model.

> The people here are taught to live in their small cubes, and they try to maximally contribute over the 100 years by doing the same job all the time. The Austrian market, in turn, is the place where there are a plenty of people, who are able to "color the cubes in blue only." One can only give a try to find a one among these people, who could color a cube into a red. They would rather color the cube blue for another 300 years, than color one cube in red.

> This is what I mean, when I say that if you try to live here, you would not integrate. If you are a foreigner with medium level of financial resources, education, capital and anything else, there is practically no possibility to integrate into this structure. (Personal communication, February 2020)

Therefore, the statement made by a post-Soviet immigrant entrepreneur in Austria supports the theory of transnational immigrant business (Ren & Liu, 2015), which suggests that the transfer of innovation and technology by immigrant entrepreneurs depends on the efficiency of the host country's bureaucracy. In the case of Austria, the bureaucracy and economic model appear to hinder the transfer and scalability of immigrant businesses, implying that the Schumpeterian type of immigrant entrepreneurship may not be expectable in CMEs. Additionally, some small Austria-based Russian-language online media, despite operating from Austria, target global Russian-speaking communities and serve as small but global businesses, emphasizing the significance of transnationalism in post-Soviet immigrant entrepreneurship in Austria, particularly since 2014. On the other hand, the partner of a Vienna-based attorney-at-law office reports a lack of knowledge about the Austrian market among post-Soviet entrepreneurs in the country.

> For many post-Soviet citizens, the biggest dream was to own a small hotel in Austrian Alps. Many of them were purchasing such small hotels, but without even basic understanding that without a good knowledge of German language, it is not easy to operate them. … If you do not speak a language, you will not be able to understand any rules and laws. …An interpreter will not always provide a correct information or an adequate translation. In addition to it, many people are not ready to work twenty-four hours a day. As a result, these hotels turn to be unprofitable. … People …think simple—to hire a managing director and based on that to receive the license. However, they do not understand how much in reality they have to pay to make operations of the business possible. They do not understand what kind of products and services are in demand in the Austrian market. They make their decisions too quickly, and such business activities usually end up very bad. (Personal communication, February 2020)

Therefore, the success and longevity of immigrant businesses in Austria are largely influenced by the professional and language proficiency of immigrant entrepreneurs, as well as their understanding of the local market, including the taxation system.

3.5 Conclusions: The Role of Entrepreneurship in Integration of Post-Soviet Immigrants in Austria

This chapter has revealed an empirical paradox in the immigrant entrepreneurship in Austria. On one hand, the legal and economic stability and the need for immigrant labor attract a relatively large number of immigrants. On the other hand, the coordination between market and non market actors and highly regulated bureaucracy in Austria to some extent presents an obstacle to the the scalability and growth of post-Soviet immigrant entrepreneurship, innovation, and technology transfer between Austria and their home countries. This supports the argument made by Dilli et al. (2018) that while CMEs are characterized by well-regulated labor markets and reliable legal systems that support inter-firm collaborations, they do not translate into the creation of Schumpeterian ventures. The coordination between business and state in Austria also leaves little room for newcomers and immigrants, resulting in socioeconomic marginalization, whether at the low or high margins. In exceptional cases, such as some first-generation Chechen male refugees, this marginalization combined with migrants' cultural customs led to criminal activities generating gray economies (Molodikova, 2019).

While some post-Soviet citizens in Austria have received Austrian citizenship, most have not fully integrated into the local Austrian society, with many remaining within post-Soviet immigrant communities. This marginalization is further evident in the labor market, where post-Soviet immigrants, even with high levels of German knowledge and initial qualifications, often face indirect discrimination as TCNs. The restriction on family members' right to work for the first year after arrival through family reunion visas also hinders their socioeconomic integration into Austrian society. In general, it is noted that young people tend to integrate more easily into the local Austrian society; however, this exception confirms the rule of marginalization of immigrants in CMEs. These findings emphasize the importance of addressing barriers to integration, including language and professional skills, as well as knowledge of the local market and taxation system, for the success and sustainability of immigrant entrepreneurship and integration in Austria.

Second, the majority of post-Soviet immigrants in Austria arrived through three channels: as students, established businesspeople, or marriage migrants. According to this study, the most significant factors influencing their decision to immigrate to Austria were the legal and economic stability of the Austrian system, as well as the opportunity to receive high-quality higher education at a relatively low cost. This finding is novel compared to previous works in the field of immigrant entrepreneurship, such as Portes (1997), Rath (2006), and Waldinger (2009). The latter have shown that better standards of life and the search for better employment and investment opportunities than those available in home countries were among the top motives for immigration to countries representing liberal market economies and immigration regimes. At the same time, this finding aligns with Nazareno et al. (2018) model of the embeddedness of immigrant entrepreneurship into three sets of factors in host and home countries.

The chapter also reveals that post-Soviet immigrant entrepreneurship in Austria consists of three broad types in relation to their social roles. The most frequent type is grassroots micro businesses usually operating in the form of self-employed or individual entrepreneurs. At the other end of the spectrum are immigrants who are corporation founders or established businesspeople who either change the jurisdiction of their businesses operating (at least as of 2022) in countries that were remnants of the Soviet Union or purchase and develop relatively large businesses in Austria, typically in the hospitality and construction development sectors. The third type consists of media, legal, financial, and medical services individual entrepreneurs and firms that frequently connect top-down entrepreneurs with the Austrian market, the legal system, and sometimes with bottom-up post-Soviet entrepreneurs. Table 3.3 summarizes this typology, which could be applied and tested further in other countries characterized as CMEs by the VoC framework.

This finding in Austria contradicts some previous research on post-Soviet entrepreneurship in Germany, which showed that high-tech-related

Table 3.3 Typology of post-Soviet immigrant entrepreneurship in Austria

Sectors and forms of post-Soviet entrepreneurship in Austria	*Type of immigrant entrepreneurship*
Education, retail, logistics, construction, beauty self-employed and rentals micro firms	*Grassroots* immigrant entrepreneurship
Legal, finance, media and medical services	*Connectors* to the local market and between immigrant businesses
Real estate development, hospitality—hotels	*Corporant/*investments-based entrepreneurship

projects and the search for financial support drive post-Soviet entrepreneurship in Germany (Tepavcevic, 2013). It highlights the differences between CMEs and the need for further exploration and classification of immigrant entrepreneurship within them. Similarly, the finding regarding female post-Soviet immigrant entrepreneurs in Austria contrasts with prior literature on immigrant entrepreneurship, which often assumes that entrepreneurial activities are the sole solution to limited access to the host country's labor market, or an opportunity for investments and provision of ethnic products and services (Dilli, Elert et al., 2018). However, the tendency for post-Soviet immigrant women in Austria to combine their entrepreneurial pursuits with part-time employment suggests that in CMEs where access to the local labor market and scalable entrepreneurship opportunities are limited, diversifying economic activities and sources of income is a rational solution. This finding constitutes a novel contribution to the field, highlighting the importance of considering the specificities of CMEs when studying immigrant entrepreneurship.

This fourth finding concerning post-Soviet immigrant entrepreneurship in Austria supports the relevance of the "ethnic" or common-culture-based thesis in the context of post-Soviet immigrant entrepreneurship in Austria and more broadly in countries characterized as CMEs. As post-Soviet communities have grown in number over time in Austria, there has been an increased demand for bilingual services, particularly in the legal and medical fields. Structural discrimination, as defined by Marchand and Siegel (2015), influences strong community ties among immigrants and contributes to the growth of social capital, which supports immigrant entrepreneurship (Kontos, 2003). However, the chapter also revealed that female immigrant entrepreneurs in certain legal professions in Austria have experienced gender-based discrimination, a finding that requires further investigation in other countries classified as CMEs. Additionally, as the analysis in this chapter has revealed, the success of immigrant entrepreneurship in CMEs relies heavily on the entrepreneurs' knowledge of the local market and legal system, as argued by Tirpitz et al. (2011) in their study of Russian investments in Germany. This idea is further explored in the next chapter, which focuses on post-Soviet immigrant entrepreneurship in Spain, a country characterized as a mixed market economy (MME) within the VoC framework.

References

. (2016). *Russkaja Gostinaja*. https://www.russkajagostinaja.at

. (2022). *Luxury Immibilien*. https://luxury-vienna.com/about-us

Austria Government (Producer). (2019, January 1). Federal Government's Official Information Website on Migration to Austria. *www.migration.gv.at*. https://www.migration.gv.at/en/living-and-working-in-austria/integration-and-citizenship/integration-agreement/

Baubock, R. (2006). *Migration and Citizenship. Legal Status, Rights and Political Participation*. Amsterdam University Press.

Bikova, E. (2011). Baturina pokupaet centr Vienny. *Euromag*. https://www.euromag.ru/economics/baturina-pokupaet-centr-veny/

Byford, A. (2012). The Russian Diaspora in International Relations: "Compatriots" in Britain. *Europe-Asia Studies, 64*(4), 715–735.

Dilli, S., Elert, N., & Herrmann, A. (2018). Varieties of Entrepreneurship: Exploring the Institutional Foundations of Different Entrepreneurship Types Through 'Varieties-of-Capitalism' Arguments. *Small Business Economics, 51*(2), 293–320.

Dunnecker, P., & Cakir, A. (2016). Female Migrant Entrepreneurs in Vienna: Mobility and Its Embeddedness. *Österreichische Zeitschrift für Soziologie, 41*, 97–113.

Eurostat, 2022 Real GDP Per Capita. (2022). https://ec.europa.eu. https://ec.europa.eu/eurostat/databrowser/view/tessi190/default/table?lang=en

Global Entrepreneurship Monitor (Producer). (2021). Entrepreneurial Behaviour and Attitudes, Austria. https://www.gemconsortium.org/economy-profiles/austria-2

Huddleston, T., Niessen, J., Ni Chaoimh, E., & White, E. (2011). *Migrant Integration Policy Index II*. The British Council and Migration Policy Group.

Kontos, M. (2003). Self-employment Policies and Migrants' Entrepreneurship in Germany. *Entrepreneurship and Regional Development, 15*(2), 119–135.

Kraler, A. (2011). The Case of Austria. In *Migration Policymaking in Europe. The Dynamics of Actors and Contexts in Past and Present*. Amsterdam University Press, IMSCOE.

Light, I. (1984). Immigrant and Ethnic Enterprise in North America. *Ethnic and Racial Studies, 7*(2), 195–216.

Marchand, K., & Siegel, M. (2015). *World Migration Report 2015: Immigrant Entrepreneurship in Cities – Background Paper*.

Molodikova, I. (2019). Muslim Refugees from Russia: Do the Chechens Bring Their Own "aul" from Chechnya to the EU? In *In Muslim Minorities and the Refugee Crisis in Europe. Narratives and Policy Responses* (p. 339). SGH.

Nazareno, J., Zhou, M., & You, T. (2018). Global Dynamics of Immigrant Entrepreneurship. Changing Trends, Ethnonational Variations, and Reconceptualizations. *International Journal of Entrepreneurial Behavior & Research*.

New Viennese Journal. (2020, May). https://nwm.at/nvz/archive

Perchinig, B. (2013). *10 Observations on the Future of Migration: Costs, Benefits and Policy Responses.*

Portes, A. (1997). *Globalization from Below: The Rise of Transnational Communities.* Princeton University.

"Pravda" Program. (2016, October 24).

Rath, J. (2006). *Entrepreneurship Among Migrants and Returnees: Creating New Opportunities*, Turin.

Ren, N., & Liu, H. (2015). Traversing Between Transnationalism and Integration: Dual Embeddedness of New Chinese Immigrant Entrepreneurs in Singapore. *Asian and Pacific Migration Journal, 24*(3), 298–326.

Shvarts, A. (2010). Elite Entrepreneurs from the Former Soviet Union: How They Made Their Millions. PhD Dissertation.

Statistics Austria – Migration. (2021–2022). https://www.statistik.at/en/statistics/population-and-society/population/migration-and-naturalisation/migration-total

Szczepanikova, A. (2008). Settlement and (re) construction of Gender Relations in Exile: Chechen Refugees in Eastern Europe in Chechens in the European Union. In A. Janda, L. Norbert, & V. Mathias (Eds.), *Chechens in the European Union.* Österreichischer Integrationfonds (Federal Ministry of Interior).

Tepavcevic, S. (2013). Russian Foreign Policy and Outward Foreign Direct Investments: Cooperation, Subordination, or Disengagement? Ph.D. Dissertation.

Tepavcevic, S. (2018). In the Bear's Shadow? Russia's International Image and Its Influence on Investments of Russian Companies in Post-Socialist Europe. *Journal of East-West Business, 24*(2), 108–137.

Tirpitz, A., Groll, C., & Ghane, K. (2011). *Russian Companies Enter Germany.*

TVRain. (2019, October). Hard Days Night.

Van Mol, C., & de Valk, H. (2016). Migration and Immigrants in Europe: A Historical and Demographic Perspective. In *Integration Processes and Policies in Europe* (pp. 31–55). Springer.

Waldinger, R. (2009). Beyond Transnationalism: An Alternative Perspective on Immigrants' Homeland Connections. In *Oxford Handbook of the Politics of International Relations* (pp. 74–102). Oxford University Press.

World Bank National Accounts Data, Austria GDP Growth. (2022). *www.worldbank.org.* https://data.worldbank.org/indicator/NY.GDP.MKTP.KD.ZG?locations=AT

CHAPTER 4

Post-Soviet Entrepreneurship in Mixed Market Economy: The Case of Spain

Abstract This chapter explores the role of immigrant entrepreneurship in the integration of post-Soviet immigrants in Spain by examining the development of the Spanish institutional system. According to the Varieties of Capitalism framework, this system is characterized as a mixed market economy (MME)—a combination of liberal and coordinated market economies—and as an Extra-Union type of immigration regime. The findings show that similar to the Austrian context of a Coordinated Market Economy (CME), the integration regime in Spain limits the access of post-Soviet immigrants to the labor market. However, Spain's economic modernization and dominance of certain economic sectors have prompted post-Soviet immigrants to identify and establish businesses in untapped niches in the service sector. As a result, five types of post-Soviet entrepreneurship have emerged in Spain, including grassroots entrepreneurs, connectors, and *corporants*, as well as individual middle-class and new exclusive immigrant entrepreneurs. The chapter also highlights that post-Soviet entrepreneurs in Spain tend to cooperate and integrate equally with other immigrant communities and with Spaniards.

Keywords Capitalism variety • Mixed market • Spain • Immigration regime • Post-Soviet entrepreneurship • Immigrants' integration

S. Tepavcevic, *Diversity of Migrant Entrepreneurship in Varieties of European Capitalism*,
https://doi.org/10.1007/978-3-031-31097-3_4

4.1 Introduction: The Relationship Between Spanish Economic Model and Immigration

Spain experienced the longest fascist dictatorship in Europe under General Francisco Franco from 1938 to 1975, during which the country remained mostly isolated from the rest of the world, except for Vatican City, Portugal, and Argentina, as noted by Bruquetas-Callejo et al. (2011). The country underwent a rapid transformation after Franco's death in 1975, democratizing its political system and transforming it into a market economy. In 1982, Spain joined NATO, and in 1986, it joined the European Community, leading to further stages of EU integration, including the adoption of common migration and monetary policies (Royo, 2014). Spain's rapid and successful reforms earned it recognition as an "economic miracle" and Europe's model for economic development and modernization. As a result, Spain experienced a migration reversal, turning into a country of mass immigration by the mid-1990s. Before the 2008–2013 Great Recession, Spain had one of the highest economic growths in the EU, with almost 4 percent in 2006 and 2007 respectively, and became the second-largest job creator in the EU after Germany (Royo, 2014). Under Zapatero's left-wing leadership in 2002, Spain joined the European monetary union (EMU) and adopted the Euro, like most EU member states. Both EU and EMU memberships had a positive impact on Spain's economy and society. As Royo (2014) stated,

> [I]t contributed to macroeconomic stability, it imposed fiscal discipline and central bank independence, and it lowered dramatically the cost of capital...[the transformation was] not only economic but also social ....In 2006, the active population increased by 3.5%, the highest in the EU (led by new immigrants and the incorporation of women in the labor market, which increased from 59% in 1995 to 72% in 2006); and 772,000 new jobs were created.

Spain experienced a construction and hospitality boom in the mid-2000s, driven by credit expansion from banks. At the same time, the number of immigrants reached five million (Bruquetas Cellejo et al., 2011; Royo, 2014). The 2008–2013 global economic crisis, popularly referred to as the Great Recession, caused a collapse of the real estate bubble leading to high unemployment, declining consumption, and a drop in service and manufacturing sectors, as well as an increase in household debt (Royo,

2014). The Recession revealed that Spain's economic growth was fragile with low productivity growth (only a half percentage contribution to potential GDP 1998–2006) and deteriorating competitiveness. As Royo (2014) argued,

> The growth was based on low-intensity sectors, such as services and construction, which were not exposed to international competition. In 2006, the majority of new jobs were in low-productivity sectors, such as construction (33%), housing-related services (15%), and tourism and domestic service (30%).

The global economic crisis and the bursting of the construction and real estate boom in Spain led to a sharp increase in unemployment, prompting both foreign-born and native Spaniards to emigrate in search of better opportunities (González-Ferrer & Moreno-Fuentes, 2017). Despite the lingering effects of the Great Recession and the recent economic crisis caused by the COVID-19 pandemic, Spain remains one of the largest economies in the EU (Table 4.1) and a top destination in Europe, with a high number of total arrivals each year.

As a result similar to other Southern European economies, Spain's economic model emerged as a mix of features from liberal and coordinated market economies. Its economic composition is based on low-productivity sectors such as construction and services (Economic Policy Reforms, 2014). In such Mediterranean or mixed market economies (MMEs), the state plays a crucial role in regulation and coordination, compensating for the absence of institutional complementarities (Molina & Rhodes, 2007). This gatekeeping function of the state has been characterized as distinctive but not unique in Mediterranean countries, where two different trends can be observed: the growth of "autonomous coordination" in which actors manage the economy through non-market governance and "market colonization," a process where market modes of coordination emerge and

Table 4.1 Real GDP per capita and Gini Coefficient for Spain in selected years

Year	*2010*	*2015*	*2020*
Real GDP per capita in Euro per capita	23.040	23.090	22.210
Gini Coefficient (0 = total equality, 1 = total inequality)	32.5	34.6	32.1

Source: Eurostat ("Eurostat, 2022 Real GDP per capita," 2022)

prevail (Molina & Rhodes, 2007). In this way, Galletti (2018, p. 223) posits, major difference between MMEs and CMEs lays in the fragmentation among socioeconomic agents: "employers and employee organizations both in longitudinal terms (small vs. large enterprises) and in sectoral ones (public vs. private sectors)." This fragmentation in MMEs is the ultimate reason for the state's role as a gatekeeper, as it makes bottom-up coordination difficult to achieve (Galletti, 2018). Similarly, during the Great Recession, the social protection system in Spain operated as a buffer for unemployed workers, partly compensating for the loss of salaries (González-Ferrer & Moreno-Fuentes, 2017).

The remainder of the present chapter traces the emergence, development, and entrepreneurship of post-Soviet communities in Spain. Given the institutional context in Spain, the chapter is led by the question of what role does entrepreneurship play in the integration of post-Soviet immigrants in Spain. The chapter, thus, explores the relationship between MME and immigration regime (the next section), emergence of post-Soviet immigrant communities in Spain (Sect. 4.3), and types and forms of post-Soviet immigrant entrepreneurship in Spain (Sect. 4.4). The last section reviews the findings of the chapter in relation to the role of entrepreneurship in integration of post-Soviet immigrants in Spain.

4.2 The Spanish Immigration and Integration Regime

According to Allgauer (2011) and Bruquetas Cellejo et al. (2011), after the death of General Franco, Spain transformed from a traditional emigration country to a country of net immigration between the mid-1970s and the end of the 1990s. The Spanish Socialist Workers' Party's Prime Minister, Zapatero, implemented an integration-oriented migration policy, which included an amnesty for 700,000 illegal immigrants and allowed the children of Spanish expatriates from the civil war to receive Spanish citizenship. By the early 2000s, around 280,000 immigrants had settled in Spain. The nature of Spanish immigration policies has been subject to change depending on the political party in power, with more liberal policies under the leadership of the left-wing Spanish Socialist Workers' Party (PSOE) and more restrictive and conservative policies under the leadership of the right-wing People's Party (PP).

Immigration to Spain saw a significant increase in the 2000s, when the foreign population in the country rose from one million to nearly six million within a decade (González-Ferrer & Moreno-Fuentes, 2017). As Royo (2014) noted, Spain became a popular destination for European workers during this time, with over 645,000 settlers in 2004 and 500,000 in 2006. This made Spain the largest recipient of immigrants in the European Union, with these immigrants representing 10 percent of the contributors to the Social Security system. The large influx of immigrants was seen to have made a significant contribution to the economic success of Spain during the decade. The influx of immigrants increased the supply of labor, raised demand through their spending, moderated wages, put downward pressure on inflation, boosted output, and allowed the labor market to avoid labor shortages. The immigrants also contributed to consumption and brought more flexibility to the economy through their mobility and willingness to take on low-paid jobs in sectors such as construction and agriculture (Royo, 2014).

As displayed in Table 4.2, Spain has implemented several integration policy documents since 2011. Political mechanisms such as quotas and contingents influenced the integration of immigrants into the Spanish job market, which led to a concentration of immigrants in certain sectors, including housework, care work, agriculture, construction, and tourism (Allgauer, 2011). These sectors were further segregated based on the origin and gender of the immigrants. The Spanish job market overall has marked significant regional disparities, a dominant role of tertiary sectors, and a significant presence of illegal employment.

Unlike Latin American immigrants, who were granted Spanish citizenship in 1998 due to their connections with former Spanish colonies, third-country nationals (TCNs) face difficulties in acquiring citizenship in Spain Allgauer (2011). TCNs, including most immigrants from post-Soviet republics in Spain, also do not receive the same favorable treatment as immigrants from neighboring countries such as Morocco. In the MIPEX index, Huddleston et al. (2011) indicate shortcomings in the areas of citizenship and naturalization, with long and arbitrary processes requiring ten years of legal residency, unless the immigrant is from a former Spanish colony. Because of these discriminative immigration policies, the UN Committee on the Elimination of Racial Discrimination reproached Spain in 2011, and the state welcomed the application of anti-discrimination laws. However, the resources for the implementation were scarce. In addition, asylum policy played a minor role because of the restrictive system in

Table 4.2 Developments in Spanish immigration regime 1976–2022

Significant regulation/year	*Aim*	*Outcome*
Spanish nationality law/ since the late 1800s	*Jus sanguinis*—citizenship translates from parents to children	After legally residing in Spain for ten years, a foreigner can apply for the citizenship; exceptions for immigrants from Brazil, Portugal, Andorra, and former Latin American Spanish colonies, and Spanish Sephardic Jews—only two years legal residence in Spain required for citizenship
The (first) Foreigners Law 1985	Recognized fundamental rights—to life, freedom of expression and judicial guarantees regardless of the legal situation in the country	No political rights, except participation in the local elections
Resolution to organize regularization and administration of foreigners' integration/1991	To help immigrant families to reunite, quotas for labor market	120,000 applications of undocumented immigrants, most led to resident permits
The Law of Asylum/1994	To protect refugees	
Royal Decree/1996	Renewal and update is to facilitate the incorporation of foreign workers (very necessary for the country's economy) into the work field	
Second Foreigners Law/1999	Instrumentation of labor market policy on new entry	
GRECO Plan/2000	Federal coordination of integration—quotas and restriction	Increased numbers of low-skilled workers in rapidly developing low-production sectors (construction, hospitality)
2000/4 Foreigners Act (later abandoned by PP's Mariano Rajoy, and not successfully restored by PSOE's Pedro Sanchez after reform in 2018)	To include foreigners and undocumented immigrants to the healthcare system	Entitled foreign residents to full healthcare coverage regardless of their legal status, making the Spanish healthcare system the most inclusive in Europe (Bruquetas-Callejo & Perna, 2020)
2022 New Foreigners Law	To facilitate hiring of high-skilled foreigners and their social integration in Spain	At the stage of implementation as of 2022–2023

use, which prompted many political refugees to enter Spain as migrant workers (Allgauer, 2011).

Also, integration in Spain is defined as a reciprocal process between immigrants and the host society and is the responsibility of the autonomous regions, although the Spanish central government has developed a "'strategic plan for citizenship and integration' from 2007 to 2010 to guide regional policies" (Allgauer, 2011, p. 199). Since 2008, the Spanish Ministry of Labor and Migration has been responsible for immigrant employment. The unions also consider immigrants to be workers that they represent due to the demands of the Spanish labor market, particularly in low-income sectors in the shadow economy. Still, Ballester et al. (2015) observed that young and middle-aged immigrants continued to fill the needs of low-skill labor-intensive sectors and temporarily ensured the sustainability of the Spanish public pension system.

The Great Recession represented a serious challenge to both the Spanish economic model and the gradually liberalizing immigration regime. In Spain, the number of permanent immigrants dropped by more than half between 2007 and 2009, while temporary immigrants dropped by over 90 percent. Nevertheless, though in smaller numbers, the immigration of TCNs in the country continued. Total legal inflows of non-EU foreigners decreased from almost 400,000 in 2008 to half that figure in 2016 (González-Ferrer & Moreno-Fuentes, 2017). Overall, the Great Recession resulted in three significant migration-related outcomes in and from Spain. Firstly, there was a significant rise in permanent emigration to the UK. Secondly, young Spaniards temporarily migrated to Germany and France, primarily for enhancing their education and professional skills. Finally, Latin American immigrants who had acquired Spanish citizenship re-migrated to their home countries (González-Ferrer & Moreno-Fuentes, 2017).

According to the latest Migrant Refugees' Spain's country profile (*Migrants Refugees—country profile Spain*, 2020), most immigrants in Spain still come from Latin American countries and Morocco, and they mostly work in low-skill, blue-collar industries. This supports the argument made by Bruquetas Cellejo et al. (2011) that despite changes in immigration laws and regulations, Spain has yet to resolve the mismatch between its restrictive entry policies and labor demands. This has resulted in an irregular immigration model and the implementation of frequent regularization measures to address the growing number of irregular migrants (Bruquetas Cellejo et al., 2011). Overall, Spain's immigration regime evolved from being highly restrictive throughout the 1990s and 2000s to being semi-neoliberal at the beginning of 2022. The latest developments in the Spanish immigration regime appear slightly more liberal than the Extra-Union subtype, under which Boucher and Gest (2018) classified Spain. The next section examines the paths of immigration and emergence of post-Soviet immigrant communities in Spain.

4.3 Post-Soviet Communities in Spain: Motives and Paths of Immigration

By the 1990s, diaspora communities of the peoples from the former Soviet Union (FSU) were not present in the countries of Southern Europe (Khanenko-Friesen, 2017). The first immigrants from the FSU arrived in Spain in the 1990s, including some who were the descendants of "Soviet Spaniards" who had moved to the FSU after the Spanish Civil War (1936–1938) and the defeat of the Second Republic by General Franco's army. As part of the Spanish government's repatriation program implemented in the early 1990s, many of these early post-Soviet immigrants received Spanish citizenship under the *jus sanguinis* naturalization policy (Artyunov, 2017).

The immigration of people from the former Soviet Union to Spain peaked in the early 2000s. According to information from Spain-based Russian-language media, in 2020 there were officially over 80,000 Russian citizens, 107,000 Ukrainian citizens, 20,000 Moldovans, and 6000 Belarussians residing in Spain ("Barcelona.ru," 2020). However, the same sources reveal that the actual number of illegal post-Soviet immigrants in Spain was much higher, even during the COVID-19 pandemic. The largest post-Soviet immigrant communities emerged in the southeast provinces of Valencia and Murcia, as well as cities across Andalusia ("Barcelona.ru," 2020). Catalonia also hosted a relatively large post-Soviet community, including a significant Ukrainian community represented by the official Association *Chervona Kalyna* (Red Raspberry, n.d.). The association also established a Ukrainian school in Barcelona that provides teaching in Ukrainian and Spanish. Additionally, results of monitoring Russian-speaking digital communities since 2018 suggest that a large post-Soviet community has emerged in Madrid, as many Russian-speaking immigrants have relocated from coastal cities to the Spanish capital. While the overall post-Soviet immigration community across Spain is estimated to be around half a million people, studies on these communities are scarce and mainly focus on the topic of the role of migrant communities in foreign policies of post-Soviet countries (see, for example, Ershov and Gadzieva (2018) and for cultural identity, Khanenko-Friesen (2017)).

According to data gathered through personal communication and digital ethnography, the first wave of post-Soviet immigration to Spain was in the 1990s. It comprised labor migrants who came to Spain in response to the political and economic changes in their home countries. This wave of immigration coincided with Spain's transformation into a country of increasing immigration. The majority of these first post-Soviet immigrants were between the ages of eighteen and twenty-five, primarily from the southern regions of Russia and Ukraine, with vocational training and middle-level professional skills (personal communication, July 2018). They predominantly worked in the growing Spanish construction sector as blue-collar foreign workers.

> My husband was already an immigrant worker in Spain when we met. He invited me to join him here. I fell in love with the country from the first sight and learned the language quite quickly... the legal status for immigrants is the biggest challenge here and non-EU migrants are very limited in their options for integration here... I follow Spanish immigration regulations and provide newcomers with interpretation, translation, and consulting. (Personal communication, December 2019)

As Spain's migration policy changed, many of these immigrants went through various migration statuses, starting from illegal and ending in acquiring Spanish citizenship (online communication, January 2020). The mass phenomenon of post-Soviet immigration to Spain occurred in the early 2000s, when Spain initially attracted these citizens as tourists. Many of these relatively wealthy individuals purchased property in Spain and used it as a vacation home, later relocating to Spain and starting small businesses (online communication, February 2020). The largest numbers of this wave of post-Soviet immigrants settled along the coast of the Costa Blanca region, with the largest communities in Alicante and Torrevieja. Relatively large communities also emerged in the Andalusia province, especially in Malaga, where the branch of the Russian Museum operates and displays exhibitions of famous Russian and former Soviet artists. Another significant post-Soviet immigrant community emerged in Catalonia, mostly in Barcelona (online communication, February 2020).

In the towns of Alicante and Torrevieja, the post-Soviet immigrant community became highly visible due to its size. With a population of around 400,000 in Alicante concentrated in a relatively small geographical area along the Mediterranean coast, the community of approximately 50,000 Russian speakers became noticeable. Additionally, a Russian-language radio station was launched in the region and existed for a number of years (personal communication, January 2015). The website *Ispaniya po-Russki* (Spain-in-Russian), established in 1997 and with an office located in Barcelona, serves as the main mass media for the post-Soviet immigrant community in Spain ("Espana Rusa," 2020). The website includes a lifestyle magazine, *Russian Inn Spain*, which covers topics related to business, fashion, and beauty and relies on advertisements from various mostly post-Soviet businesses in Spain and across the EU. Both *Ispaniya Po-Russki* and *Russian Inn Spain* are owned by the real estate agency Ventura, owned by Elena Romanova, who is considered one of the key informal leaders of the Russian immigrant community in Spain. These examples align with Portes and Sensenbrenner's (1993) thesis that social capital is linked to a strong sense of community and the experience of "foreignness."

The official associations of post-Soviet citizens in Spain are limited in number, but social media groups centered on various aspects of life in Spain, such as "Working in Spain" and "Immigration to Spain," have taken on much of their function. Two Russian Orthodox churches, one in Madrid and another in Valencia, serve as communal gathering places for many members of the post-Soviet immigrant community (personal communication, July 2018). The massive scale of post-Soviet immigration in Spain can also be inferred from the discussions on social media groups, where participants jokingly refer to Spanish cities with Soviet-style names like "*Alicantovo*" and "*Torreviekhino*" or "*Malagino.*" There are also the Russian Association in Alicante and the Association of Russian Speakers *Nash Dom* (Our Home) in Marbella that formally represent the post-Soviet immigrant community in Spain (personal communication, July 2018).

The motivations behind immigration to Spain are diverse and can vary greatly from person to person. However, based on online research and personal conversations, some of the most commonly cited reasons include the significant difference in real estate prices between major cities in the post-Soviet region and Spanish coastal cities, where prices were among the most affordable in Europe (Kuznetsov, 2007). Other reasons cited include the desire to escape the harsh continental climate in their home countries for a more temperate Mediterranean climate that offers both emotional and health benefits (personal communication, June 2018). For example, a young Russian-speaking couple in Valencia, who was interviewed, described their typical decision-making process and journey of immigration from the post-Soviet region to Spain over the last decade.

> We had not much to lose leaving Ukraine: the country is poor so are the institutions, we rented the flat in Kyiv, it was expensive and not particularly cozy. We heard from the friends that Spain is sunny and relatively cheap. First, we came as tourists to test the terrain, and the country and the people impressed us. Everyone was so relaxed and nice, and we wanted to stay immediately. When we returned to Ukraine, we started to look for possibilities to go to Spain for longer. We got longer tourist visa, and got in touch with the friends of the friends who already lived in Valencia. We lived with them for the initial period and we shared the costs. Then they bought a flat, and we stayed in the rented flat, but we already knew a bit of Spanish and found some part-time jobs, so we could sustain ourselves financially. However, we are illegal immigrants: our visas expired, and we got some Spanish document that allows us to stay here while waiting for residence permit, but we cannot travel anywhere abroad. (Personal conversation, July 2018)

Spain was also a desirable destination for post-Soviet immigrants who lived in other EU member states, particularly Germany and Poland. For skilled labor TCN professionals, additional exams are often necessary to obtain a license to work in Spain. In post-Soviet job-searching Facebook groups, where both employers and entrepreneurs post job listings or search for employees, a comment exemplifies the views of post-Soviet immigrants on accessing the Spanish labor market and the strategies they adopt to overcome these challenges.

> If you want to work in Spain, you need to get a diploma in Spain, because the Spaniards do not trust any foreign diplomas. Before getting a job as a sport trainer in swimming, or even to work as the swimming pool watch, one needs to pass courses: first the course on emergency help on land, then in water. Regarding canteens ... without your own capital, you can wash dishes in someone else's restaurant. If you come with a lot of money, you can buy your own restaurant, but the competence is extensive! In Spain, you spit and you end up in a bar or in a restaurant. ... I have lived in Spain since

1996 and have been working in London for twelve years, because in Spain, there is work, but there is no salary! (Online discussion, September 2022)

This example reflects on the Spanish state's protection of the labor market through education qualifications and subsequently coincides with Galletti's (2018) argument about the state as a "gatekeeper" in MMEs. While mostly bearing a mutual-help character, the discussions on social media among post-Soviet immigrants in Spain (as well as in Austria as observed in the previous chapter) evolve around the advantages and disadvantages of immigration, mostly concerning the access to labor market. In that sense, the immigrants usually divide into two camps that they define as optimists and realists (or latter as pessimists), as the following example demonstrates.

I helped many our migrants in Spain! Many years ago, in a park, in a tent, a Muscovite couple and a person from Belarus lived together, and I took them home with me. There was also an urologist from Russia, the musician couple from Ukraine, and I can continue the list indefinitely! I always say that, if there is a need or desire, one can and should change her life at any age; at the end of the day, we were born with legs, not with roots! Still, before deciding to move to another country, you should at least read the news about this country through Google translator. Then your questions about the finding a job with Russian or Ukrainian certificates in Spain will disappear. (Social media discussion, October 2022)

Dissatisfaction with the regulations in Spain has also been frequently expressed in personal communication with post-Soviet entrepreneurs residing in Valencia.

The state's protection of human life here results in a paradox: human life is considered the highest value, even if it represents a threat to other humans, for example in cases of robbery or violation of ownership rights. For instance, real estate owners cannot remove occupiers from their property if the latter do not have another place to live. Although we comply with the laws, I feel unprotected here. (Online communication, June 2022)

Similar disappointment with the medical services available in Spain is shared among post-Soviet immigrants in Facebook and Telegram groups. The discussions reveal that medical services in Russian language are scarce because non-EU certificates are not recognized. Another reason for this situation is the 2018 reform of the medical system in Spain, which previously allowed all residents of Spain to use medical services equally, regardless of their legal status (Bruquetas-Callejo & Perna, 2020). As a result, Spain was considered to have some of the best medical services globally. However, being excluded as a foreigner from these services has prompted some post-Soviet migrants to leave Spain for other host countries. As one member of such groups put it, "I lived in Spain for three years, and I disliked it. It's good for a holiday, not for immigration" (online discussion, October 2022).

Therefore, with regard to Gallietti's (2018) notion of the "gatekeeper" role of the state in MMEs, in Spain, state regulations play this role by protecting the skilled labor market for locals and EU citizens while limiting access for TCN immigrants. As noted in personal communication from December 2019, many post-Soviet immigrants, particularly those with higher education and in the age range between twenty-five and forty, continue trying to learn Spanish at least to the minimum required EU A1 level and pass additional exams to have their certificates recognized in Spain. This trend became even more prevalent after the full-scale invasion of Russia in Ukraine in February 2022, which prompted not only a large number of Ukrainian citizens but also a significant number of Russian citizens to escape the war, mobilization, political prosecution, and other life-threatening situations in their countries of origin. As one participant of a social media discussion stated, "I have a high education diploma in telecommunications and extensive international experience in the field (in Ukraine and Poland). I am ready to accept any job, including olive collection" (online discussion, October 2022). As a result, many recent immigrants work at existing post-Soviet-owned businesses in Spain. The types and forms of these businesses are the subject of the following section.

4.4 Classification of Post-Soviet Entrepreneurship in Spain

Post-Soviet immigration in Spain saw the parallel emergence of post-Soviet entrepreneurship. Its classification is based on the combination of the place in the host country's market reflected in the size and sector of entrepreneurship, the relation of entrepreneurship to the post-Soviet immigrant community, and the role of entrepreneurship in immigrants' integration in a host country. Many post-Soviet immigrants who had worked as blue-collar workers in the construction sector for several years registered their activity as individual entrepreneurs and continued to work independently. They often joined forces with other post-Soviet entrepreneurs whose skills and experience complemented their own in the provision of construction services. Such collaboration was evident in all Spanish cities with significant post-Soviet communities, as seen in the advertisements in social media groups. Even in the midst of the Russian government's invasion of Ukraine in late 2022, immigrants from Russia, Ukraine, and Belarus formed such joint working groups and offered their services to both locals and their compatriots living in the vicinity of their residences in Spain. This collaboration among citizens of warring countries demonstrates their limited access to the labor market, as well as the strengthening of communication channels among the immigrant community, as suggested by Marchand and Siegel (2015) concerning structural discrimination toward TCNs. However, these groups sometimes experienced internal conflicts. Illegal post-Soviet immigrants also joined these groups in search of a regular income and to legalize their status through employment contracts. Between 2014 and 2022, illegal post-Soviet immigrants in Spain consisted of both Ukrainian and Russian citizens who initially arrived as tourists and stayed beyond their visa-free period for Ukrainians or tourist visas for Russians. However, following Russia's full-fledged invasion of Ukraine in 2022, only Russian citizens remained as illegal immigrants. Given the informal nature of these agreements, established immigrant entrepreneurs sometimes capitalized on the vulnerability of the illegal status of their compatriots, paying them less than initially agreed, which occasionally led to a lack of solidarity and generosity within the post-Soviet immigrant community in Spain (personal communication, February 2019).

The early post-Soviet immigrants, mostly women, in Spain also established entrepreneurship in domestic services, hospitality, and agriculture. They worked as *autonomo* (individual entrepreneur or self-employed), often earning lower wages and having higher levels of temporality compared to native entrepreneurs. They frequently held multiple jobs, including translation, legal, and financial services for post-Soviet investors who immigrated after 2000. Being small in size and scale and fulfilling the primary economic role in integration of post-Soviet immigrants, this group represents a grassroots type of immigrant entrepreneurship. It also served as the foundation for current post-Soviet-owned micro-reconstruction and medium-sized construction companies in Spain. For each subsequent wave of post-Soviet immigration, these groups and companies provided first employment or services to post-Soviet real estate buyers and business investors.

In the late 1990s and early 2000s, Russian-language media were established by post-Soviet immigrants in Alicante and Barcelona, where most Russian-speaking immigrant communities were concentrated. Unlike the post-Soviet micro-construction companies, the Russian-language radio in Alicante initially represented an example of "ethnic" entrepreneurship, according to Portes (1997), or common-culture-based entrepreneurship, as described by Tepavcevic (2021). Both its suppliers and customers were post-Soviet, Russian-speaking immigrants, and the radio earned revenue from advertisements for products and services catering to the needs and interests of this group. However, with the rise of digital social media and the impact of the Great Recession, the radio's advertisement potential declined (as reported in a personal communication in January 2015).

Another Russian-language media, the aforementioned Spain-in-Russian initially founded as a real estate agency, eventually became a business that served the post-Soviet immigrant community, with other immigrants and community-oriented businesses as clients. As travel from the former Soviet Union to Spain increased, the company expanded its services to include tourism. Recognizing the growing interest among the population of FSU countries in immigrating to Spain, the founders established a representation in Russia, the largest and wealthiest among the former Soviet markets (at least by 2022), making it a classic example of simultaneous embeddedness immigrant entrepreneurship as defined by Nazareno et al. (2018). In addition to its geographic expansion to Russia, the portal has diversified its services to include a range of offerings, including legal and education consulting, real estate agency services, and logistics. This diversification has allowed Spain-in-Russian to continue to operate during and after the Great Recession and the recent COVID-19 pandemic, and it continues to function and hire post-Soviet immigrants throughout Spain.

During the 2000s, post-Soviet citizens visiting Spain started to purchase real estate more frequently. According to scholars studying outward foreign direct investments from former Soviet countries, these purchases were partially for vacations, but the real motivation behind them was to escape from the dysfunctional economic and political institutions of their home countries (Liuhto, 2005) and create "additional airports" abroad (Kuznetsov, 2007). To overcome the restrictions of the Spanish immigration regime, these post-Soviet immigrants often registered companies in

Spain and conducted businesses in the real estate trade and construction, providing themselves with residence permits in the process. In some cases, their children saw Spain as their home and moved there to study, and after graduation, they established their own businesses as lawyers specializing in migration and real estate purchases (personal communication, January 2015).

The growth of post-Soviet immigrant communities in Spain became evident through the proliferation of retail shops selling products related to post-Soviet cuisine and souvenirs. These shops were mainly established in Catalonia and Costa Blanca, but also in large cities in Andalusia. The first wave of post-Soviet immigrants founded and operated these retail shops, such as the shop "Siberia-Slavic products in Barcelona" targeting post-Soviet immigrant community both by name and by credo. Along with retail shops, post-Soviet-founded educational centers also emerged in Spanish cities and resorts where many post-Soviet immigrants are concentrated. These Russian-founded private schools, which offer Russian language and music classes, are examples of common-culture-based immigrant businesses. These Russian-founded private schools usually offer Russian language and music classes, and their names reflect their mission in children's education: *Planeta Znaniy* (The Planet of Knowledge), *Slovo* (The Word), and *Malen'kie Genii* (Small Geniuses), to name a few. They cooperate with non-governmental local associations of compatriots (personal communication, December 2019). Their geographical locations suggest that the largest Russian-speaking communities are in Catalonia, counting even six schools of additional education. They cooperate with local non-governmental associations of compatriots and are in Catalonia, Valencia, Andalusia, Madrid, Castella and Leon, Navarra, Canarias, and Rioja ("Espana Rusa," 2020). In total, there are nineteen such centers of additional education where post-Soviet immigrants serve as customers and entrepreneurs.

One such school was founded in 2013 by three female language and legal professionals who came to study in Spain. Initially, the school was named *Matryoshka* (Nested Doll) and offered courses in Russian and Spanish languages, serving mainly post-Soviet immigrants. The school later rebranded to FreeDa, reflecting its aim to become more multicultural and incorporating English courses into its portfolio. Thus, following the entrepreneurial expression, after validation among the post-Soviet immigrant community, the school continued to grow toward local and global customers offering and applying innovative methods. The special language acquisition method was developed through the school's continuous growth and adaptation to the needs of its students. In 2017, the school was approved for Cervantes Institute accreditation. As stated on the school's website, "We continue to grow with all the people around us, studying our students and their needs, studying different manuals and methods" ("FreeDa Language Space," 2017). The school employs sixteen professionals with administrative staff and some language teachers coming mostly from Russia and the rest are local Spaniards and Catalans. The school has formed partnerships with other language schools in Spain and other EU countries and is planning to open a second location in Barcelona. The school also serves as a connector between the Russian-speaking community and the education system in Spain. The founders stated that they established the cooperation with other language schools in the Spanish region of Andalusia, as well as with some schools in other EU countries (online communication, December 2022). They also officially announced the opening of one more school in another location in Barcelona. These statements suggest that at least in the education sector, Spanish economic model encourages certain innovation and cooperation among similar businesses, including immigrant-founded ones. At the same time, as stated on its website, this language school provides legal support to its customers from the FSU. Simultaneously, being usually members of compatriots' local associations, these schools serve as connectors among Russian-speaking communities across all EU member states, but also as the immigrant community's connectors to the education system of the receiving countries (personal communication, October 2018).

The largest post-Soviet immigrant-owned business in Spain is Alegria, a company founded in 2011 by Ian Veinrukh, a post-Soviet Israeli citizen. Initially a real estate agency, Alegria has diversified into construction, becoming one of the significant developer companies in the Costa Blanca region. The company offers real estate, immigration, education, and medical tourism consulting services and has a YouTube channel to provide informational support and advertise its services. However, the slow and indiscreet Spanish bureaucracy has been the only obstacle in founding and developing the business, according to the company's founder (online communication, November 2022). The company develops projects with "smart home"' technology; however, according to the company's owner, the real estate business is mostly oriented to foreigners because "Spaniards are quite conservative and it takes five to seven years to accept some technological novelty" ("Alegria," 2010–2023). According to the company's founder, "the only obstacle in founding and developing business has been related to Spanish bureaucracy, traditionally slow and indiscrete. As a result, we make plans for investments in projects, but they realize with significant delay" ("RussianInn," 2019, p. 59).

The rapid growth of the company is reflected in its expanding offices and workforce, which now numbers between sixty and eighty employees, including a majority from the former Soviet Union, as well as Britons and Spaniards. As stated on its website (in Russian), the company seeks to "develop social infrastructure for the region and create a cosmopolitan environment that is comfortable for foreign investment and life on the Spanish coast" ("Alegria," 2010–2023). This goal aligns with liberalization of Spain's immigration policy prompted by the Great Recession in 2013 to offer residency permits to non-EU citizens who invested over 500,000 Euro in the country. Most recipients of these "golden residence permits" in Spain have been Russian and Chinese citizens, looking not only for residency but also for stable investment opportunities (personal communication, January 2015). With services provided in clients' native languages and participation in charity projects and events of local and immigrant communities, Alegria and Spain-in-Russian are helping to consolidate the post-Soviet immigrant community in Spain. This consolidation of post-Soviet communities constitutes a corporation-like immigrant entrepreneurship, or "corporant" type of post-Soviet immigrant entrepreneurship in Spain.

In the period between 2005 and 2019 in Alicante, other two post-Soviet Russian-speaking immigrants founded high-tech businesses. The first is solar batteries plants Solbisco, functioning as a part of the Immodo Group. The founder and owner, Alexander Tetyukhin, who came from Latvia to Spain in 2005, points out that the Solbisco plants are the first solar batteries plants in Spain that are built without EU donations. In his words,

> The time dictates the actuality of this business, because of worldwide ecological and alternative sources of energy significantly reduce air pollution. For example, one of my plants reduced up to 2100 tons of carbon dioxide. Today, such projects are in demand not only because they are useful for humanity, but also because they provide economic effectiveness and stability (ten percent of annual profitability during a minimum thirty years), and it is practically resilient to crises. In addition, the business does not require suppliers, materials, administrative resources, and intermediaries. Our clients

> are investors interested in high and guaranteed profitability, such as private persons, companies, and various foundation, including pension ones. ("RussianInn," 2019, p. 59)

Alexander Fyodorov is a post-Soviet immigrant who has made a significant impact on the business community in Alicante, Spain. Prior to moving to Spain, he worked as a professional financial strategist in Russia and as a trader at the New York Stock Exchange (NYSE) and NASDAQ. Fyodorov also founded the Forum of Traders and Investors in Moscow. Upon moving to Alicante, Fyodorov identified a demand for investment platforms among post-Soviet immigrants living in Spain. These immigrants often have resident permits that do not allow them to work, leading them to spend their initial savings instead of investing. Fyodorov responded to this demand by founding the Club of Investors FXDTE. Fyodorov notes that the investment market in Spain is largely uncovered, with many people investing in securities recommended by banks without proper analysis. He believes that the investment topic is secretive and that personal contacts and recommendations, as well as business events, are the most reliable platforms for acquiring clients. As he puts it, "money loves silence" ("RussianInn," 2019, p. 60).

Similar to Alegria's use of "smart home" technology, Solbisco and Club of Investors FXDTE provide high-tech services that are less knowledge-intensive. However, these businesses cater to a more specific and exclusive market, making them a separate type of new exclusive immigrant entrepreneurship. In terms of the forms of services they provide, all three companies—Alegria, Solbisco, and Club of Investors FXDTE—resemble the Schumpeterian type of entrepreneurship to some extent. Simultaneously, these two examples of post-Soviet immigrant entrepreneurship in Spain demonstrate that "disruption" is not an autonomous process but a phenomenon deeply contextualized in the intersection of geography and time.

Research through direct inquiries and social media analysis of employees of post-Soviet founded companies in Spain shows that many of them move between these businesses, and some even work part-time for multiple companies. Most of these employees have lived in Spain for a decade and a significant portion have received higher education from Spanish universities. These post-Soviet immigrants' businesses have had a significant impact on the development of the post-Soviet diaspora in Catalonia and Costa Blanca. They operate as hybrids of common-culture enclaves, mainstream local and global economies. Despite many post-Soviet immigrants in Spain having obtained higher education and substantial professional experience, they tend to have low expectations for employment in the country. As the authors of “My Spain” YouTube channel immigrant stated, “in the beginning, we continued to work for our clients in Russia remotely, but soon we realized that our earnings were not enough to cover our living costs in Spain” (“Rabota dlya nelegala,” 2021). Like post-Soviet immigrants in Austria, many recent post-Soviet immigrants in Spain aged between twenty-five and forty have created YouTube channels as either additional or the only source of income, where they share their immigrant experiences or provide instructions on how to move to Spain. Some of these immigrants have also purchased apartments in Spain, which they rent out to Spaniards and tourists.

In addition, post-Soviet immigrants have opened restaurants in coastal resorts, although they often face challenges due to the seasonal nature of the hospitality industry in Mediterranean countries. One interlocutor admitted,

> We moved to Spain and opened the restaurant in early spring, hiring local Spaniards. Wealthy Brits and French were our major customers, and the restaurant was a highly profitable business until mid-September. Then the people disappeared. We tried to attract customers by organizing various entertainment events, but soon we realized that the problem was the fact that in the colder period of the year, almost no one lives here. To avoid further losses, we had to fire employees and close the restaurant until the next warm season. (Personal conversation, October 2018)

This experience suggests that many post-Soviet immigrants do not always thoroughly research the local market before starting a business in a receiving country, which Tirpitz et al. (2011) found among Russian SMEs entering the German market. Overall, these businesses are involved in both the local mainstream economies and the global economy, constituting a separate type of post-Soviet entrepreneurship in Spain—individual middle-class entrepreneurship. Beauty services are also a frequent form of individual entrepreneurship among post-Soviet immigrants in Spain. They are found in areas with high concentrations of post-Soviet communities and are heavily advertised on social media groups. These beauty services, which usually involve self-employment and minimal investment, belong to the grassroots type of immigrant entrepreneurship.

4.5 Conclusions: The Role of Entrepreneurship in Post-Soviet Integration in Spain

The chapter has highlighted that Spain appeals to immigrants due to its large domestic market of approximately forty-two million people and its immigration policies that allow residents to stay in the country without legal status. However, institutional barriers for immigrants in Spain also exist, leading to four common paths. The first path is self-employment and entrepreneurship, which is most common among post-Soviet immigrants and usually takes a grassroots form of entrepreneurship. The second path is SME forming corporation-building immigrant, or shorter—"corporant" type of entrepreneurship. The third is further migration to other European countries. The fourth, less frequent, path is marriage to Spaniards and family-based social integration, which provides gradual access to the Spanish labor market. The post-Soviet immigrant entrepreneurship in Spain is influenced by both the dynamics between Spanish and EU regulatory discrimination of TCNs and the impact of globalization. The state regulations in Spain play a "gatekeeper" role in protecting the skilled labor market for Spanish citizens, former Spanish colonies, and EU citizens while limiting access to TCNs. This has resulted in many post-Soviet immigrants setting up companies and businesses, some of which are successful. Others exploit the relatively low costs of initial investments to start businesses, mainly in the tourism, construction, or logistics sectors, by using post-Soviet immigrants as skilled employees and service providers. These earlier post-Soviet immigrants, who have learned Spanish and integrated economically, serve as interpreters, legal advisors, and real estate agents.

The forms, size of post-Soviet immigrant entrepreneurship, and its role in immigrant integration in Spain have resulted in the emergence of four types. The first type consists of self-employed individuals and micro firms offering services in various sectors such as construction, logistics, beauty, retail, and individual interpretation and consulting services and represents grassroots type entrepreneurs. On the other hand, post-Soviet immigrants who have founded enterprises that have grown from small to medium size are mostly present in the real estate and hospitality sectors, operating as locally registered firms. These enterprises, classified as "corporants," combine the corporate nature of their businesses, immigrant ownership and investment, and human resources, and in these characteristics, they resemble their counterparts in Austria. However, in contrast to their Austrian counterparts, they also develop Russian language media, displaying further innovativeness in combining various sectors. In this way, they also integrate and consolidate immigrant communities to generate new diasporas among post-Soviet immigrants in Spain. Further research is needed to relate these findings in other countries classified as MMEs by the VoC framework (Galletti, 2018).

The specificity of Spanish MMEs has generated two additional types of post-Soviet immigrant entrepreneurship. Close to the grassroots type in form, individual middle-class immigrant entrepreneurs immigrate with their own savings and either buy apartments to rent or run their own YouTube channels, capitalizing on the number of followers and subsequent advertisements. While similar entrepreneurial activities are also present in Austria, due to Austrian regulations, they function in the form of micro companies and are classified as grassroots immigrant entrepreneurs.

Lastly, the examination of post-Soviet immigrant entrepreneurship in Spain reveals that certain post-Soviet entrepreneurial activities connect post-Soviet immigrant communities within particular localities and across Spain. In contrast to Austria, where Russian-language media play such a role, centers of additional education in Spain serve as connectors, both horizontally among themselves and vertically with other post-Soviet immigrant businesses. This role in integration and functioning of post-Soviet immigrant communities in Spain largely coincides with Portes and Sensenbrenner's (1993) thesis that social capital backs entrepreneurship, as well as Kontos' (2003) theory highlighting the significance of communication channels in strengthening immigrant communities.

Finally, for being rare examples of high-tech services, two post-Soviet founded companies located in Alicante, Solbisco and Club of Investors FXDTE, represent a distinct type of immigrant entrepreneurship labeled as the "new exclusives." These companies, aimed at different customer segments, embody a relatively new direction for private and immigrant businesses. Club of Investors FXDTE also acts as a horizontal connector among the wealthier representatives of the post-Soviet immigrant community in Spain, supporting the idea that belonging to a certain social circle is essential for economic success, as previously noted by Remennick (2012) in the context of Soviet Jews in the Soviet Union. A summary of these findings can be seen in Table 4.3.

In conclusion, the study of post-Soviet entrepreneurship in Spain supports the theory that the timing of immigration influences the type and

Table 4.3 Classification of post-Soviet immigrant entrepreneurship in Spain

Sectors and forms of post-Soviet entrepreneurship in Spain	*Type of immigrant entrepreneurship*
Retail, logistics, construction, beauty self-employed, and micro firms	*Grassroots* immigrant entrepreneurship
Apartment rentals and YouTube channels	*Individual middle-class* immigrant entrepreneurs
Additional education centers and language schools	*Connectors* of the local, Spain-based, and EU post-Soviet immigrant communities
Multisector service businesses—real estate development legal, finance, and education consulting, media, hospitality—hotels and restaurants	*Corporants*/growth-based entrepreneurship
Renewable energy, securities trade, and investment club/platform	*New exclusives* immigrant entrepreneurship

form of entrepreneurship initially proposed by Tepavcevic (2017) and Ryazantsev et al. (2018). The findings also suggest that the mixed market economy model in Spain allows for a more diverse range of immigrant entrepreneurship compared to Austrian coordinated market model. The post-Soviet immigrant entrepreneurship in Spain offers innovative services that fill some previously deficient knowledge-intensive services in this host country. Further research is needed to examine the applicability of these findings to the dependent market economy (DME) that is a much newer VoC model present in the EU. The forms and role of post-Soviet entrepreneurship in immigrants' integration in one of DMEs, Hungary, is explored in the next chapter.

References

Alegria. (2010–2023).

Allgauer, A. (2011). Debating Integration: A Comparison of Topics and Policies in Austria and Spain. In *Looming Shadows: Migration and Integration at a Time of Upheaval* (pp. 191–219). Center for Transatlantic Relations.

Artyunov, A. A. (2017). Spanish Immigrants and the Institute of Citizenship in the USSR (The Second Half of 1930s and the Beginning of 1940s). *RUDN Journal of World History, 9*(2), 132–138.

Ballester, R., Velazco, J., & Rigall-I-Torrent, R. (2015). Effects of the Great Recession on Immigrants' Household Consumption in Spain. *Social Indicators Research, 123*(3), 771–797.

Barcelona.ru. (2020). https://barcelona.ru/

Boucher, A., & Gest, J. (2018). *Crossroads: Comparative Immigration Regimes in a World of Demographic Change*. Cambridge University Press.

Bruquetas-Callejo, M., Garces-Mascarenas, B., Moren-Alegret, R., Penninx, R., & Ruiz-Vieytez, E. (2011). The Case of Spain. In *Migration Policymaking in Europe: The Dynamics of Actors and Contexts in Past and Present* (pp. 291–323). Amsterdam University Press.

Bruquetas-Callejo, M., & Perna, R. (2020). Migration and Healthcare Reforms in Spain: Symbolic Politics, Converging Outputs, Oppositions from the Field. *South European Society and Politics, 25*(1), 75–98.

Chervona Kalyna. (n.d.).

Economic Policy Reforms. (2014).

Ershov, V. F., & Gadzieva, K. K. (2018). Russian Community in Spain and Cultural Dialogue (1991–2015). *RUDN Journal of Russian History, 17*(1), 92–108.

Espana Rusa. (2020). *Espanarusa*. https://espanarusa.com/

Eurostat, 2022 Real GDP Per Capita. (2022). https://ec.europa.eu. https://ec.europa.eu/eurostat/databrowser/view/tessi190/default/table?lang=en

FreeDa Language Space. (2017). https://freedaspace.com/en/

Galletti, F. (2018). Institutions of Coordination in Mixed Market Economies: The Gatekeeper Role of the State in Labour Relations. *Sociology and Anthropology, 6*(7), 589–601.

González-Ferrer, A., & Moreno-Fuentes, F. J. (2017). Back to the Suitcase? Emigration During the Great Recession in Spain. *South European Society and Politics, 22*(4), 447–471.

Huddleston, T., Niessen, J., Ni Chaoimh, E., & White, E. (2011). *Migrant Integration Policy Index II*. British Council and Migration Policy Group.

Khanenko-Friesen, N. (2017). Migrant Self-Reflectivity and New Ukrainian Diaspora in Southern Europe: The Case of Portugal. In *Post-Soviet Migration and Diasporas. From Global Perspectives to Everyday Practices* (pp. 47–63). Springer International Publishing.

Kontos, M. (2003). Self-employment Policies and Migrants' Entrepreneurship in Germany. *Entrepreneurship and Regional Development, 15*(2), 119–135.

Kuznetsov, A. (2007). *The Internationalization of the Russian Economy: Innovative Aspect (In Russian)*. URSS.

Liuhto, K. (2005). *Expansion or Exodus: Why Do Russian Corporations Invest Abroad?* Routledge.

Marchand, K., & Siegel, M. (2015). *World Migration Report 2015: Immigrant Entrepreneurship in Cities – Background Paper*.

Migrants Refugees – Country Profile Spain. (2020).
Molina, O., & Rhodes, M. (2007). The Political Economy of Adjustment in Mixed Market Economies: A Study of Spain and Italy. In *Beyond Varieties of Capitalism* (pp. 223–252). Oxford University Press.
Nazareno, J., Zhou, M., & You, T. (2018). Global Dynamics of Immigrant Entrepreneurship. Changing Trends, Ethnonational Variations, and Reconceptualizations. *International Journal of Entrepreneurial Behavior & Research.*
Portes, A. (1997). *Globalization from Below: The Rise of Transnational Communities.* Princeton University.
Portes, A., & Sensenbrenner, J. (1993). Embeddedness and Immigration: Notes on the Social Determinants of Economic Action. *American Journal of Sociology, 98*, 1320–1350.
Remennick, L. (2012). *Russian Jews on Three Continents. Identity, Integration, and Conflict.* Transaction Publisher.
Royo, S. (2014). Institutional Degeneration and the Economic Crisis in Spain. *American Behavioral Scientist, 58*(12), 1568–1591.
. RussianInn. (2019, October).
Ryazantsev, S., Pismennaya, E., Lukyantsev, A., Sivoplyasova, S., & Khramova, M. (2018). Modern Emigration from Russia and Formation of Russian-Speaking Communities Abroad (In Russian). *World Economy and International Relations, 62*(6), 93–107.
Tepavcevic, S. (2017). Immigrant Entrepreneurship in the Post-Socialist Countries of the European Union: Motives and Patterns of Entrepreneurship of Post-Soviet Immigrants in Hungary. *Migration and Ethnic Themes, 1*, 65–92.
Tepavcevic, S. (2021). Changing Geography, Retaining the Mentality: Social and Economic Integration of Post-Soviet Immigrants in Austria and Hungary. *Review of Economic Theory and Policy, 3*, 137–154.
Tirpitz, A., Groll, C., & Ghane, K. (2011). *Russian companies enter Germany.* GCME.

CHAPTER 5

Post-Soviet Immigrant Entrepreneurship in Investments-Dependent Market Economy: The Case of Hungary

Abstract The chapter explores the dynamics of post-Soviet entrepreneurship in Hungary, tracing its emergence within the context of the country's transition from a centrally planned to a market economy. Hungary is classified as a Dependent Market Economy (DME) in the Varieties of Capitalism literature, characterized by high dependence on foreign investments. The chapter examines the various reasons for post-Soviet immigration to Hungary, including the representation of former Soviet firms, student visas, marriage migration, and employment at multinational corporations, with only a small number immigrating as intentional entrepreneurs. The changing international position and relatively low entry costs for businesses have opened up numerous opportunities for entrepreneurship, particularly in low-technology manufacturing. The *jus sanguinis* principle extended to families in Hungary's immigration regime has resulted in most post-Soviet-led businesses being integrated into both the Hungarian mainstream and the global economy. These businesses operate in a variety of sectors, including construction, logistics, food production, and hospitality, and can be classified into six types of immigrant entrepreneurship.

Keywords Dependent market • Hungary • Immigration regime • Post-Soviet entrepreneurship • Immigrants' integration • Investment

S. Tepavcevic, *Diversity of Migrant Entrepreneurship in Varieties of European Capitalism*,
https://doi.org/10.1007/978-3-031-31097-3_5

5.1 Introduction: Hungary as a Market Economy Dependent on Foreign Investments

As many scholars previously argued and the two previous chapters confirmed, institutions are dynamic phenomena that can be affected by both bottom-up local pressures (Bohle & Greskovits, 2012) and top-down global changes (Streeck & Thelen, 2005). Out of the three countries analyzed in this monograph, Hungary has seen the most rapid and visible institutional changes over the past three decades. By 1989, Hungary was a member of the Socialist bloc with a centrally planned economy and one-party system. After the fall of the Berlin Wall, pro-democratic and market-oriented reforms began, leading to the bankruptcy of many state enterprises and high levels of unemployment in the early 1990s (Csaba, 2007). However, Hungary gradually joined Western international organizations and improved its international position. In 1995, it became an OECD member; in 1999, it joined NATO along with other post-Socialist Central and Eastern European countries; and in 2004, it joined the EU as part of the Eastern EU enlargement process. In 2008, Hungary also became a member of the Schengen Agreement. This improvement in Hungary's international position and increased immigration is reflected in its economic performance, as shown in Table 5.1.

In an effort to close the economic development gap with Western Europe, along with Poland, the Czech Republic, and Slovakia, Hungary has been attracting multinational corporation (MNC) investments since the early 1990s. This was due to Hungary's educated and relatively low-cost labor force, favorable production sites, and proximity to Western Europe (King, 2007; Nölke & Vliegenthart, 2009). According to King (2007), the reliance on foreign direct investment (FDI) in corporate governance and inter-firm relations is a defining feature of this model of market economy, which he describes as "patrimonial post-communist capitalism." King (2007, p. 325) argued that the capitalist growth in this

Table 5.1 Hungary—real GDP per capita and Gini Coefficient in selected years

Year	*2010*	*2015*	*2020*
Real GDP per capita in Euro per capita	9.988	11.228	12.730
Gini Coefficient (0 = total equality, 1 = total inequality)	24.1	28.2	28.8

Source: Eurostat ("Eurostat, 2022 Real GDP per capita," 2022)

model depends "on the investment strategies of specific MNCs, the lending decisions of foreign-owned banks, and the ability to import industrial inputs and capital from, and export manufactured goods to, the core of the global capitalist economy."

Post-socialist Europe has seen a range of market economies emerge with high levels of dependence on foreign direct investment (FDI) (Feldmann, 2019; Nölke & Vliegenthart, 2009). For their notable reliance on FDI, four countries in the region constituting the Visegrad Four group (V4)—the Czech Republic, Hungary, Poland, and Slovakia—have been defined as dependent market economies (DMEs) with distinct institutional characteristics compared to Western European advanced market economies (Nölke & Vliegenthart, 2009). Hungary, in particular, has been seen as a successful transformation from a centrally planned to a market economy, attracting MNCs with its educated and low-cost labor force, production sites, and geographical proximity to Western European markets (King, 2007). Myant and Drahokoupil (2011) further found five forms of post-communist capitalism, including foreign investment-based, peripheral, oligarchic-clientelistic, order states, and remittance-based, after analyzing patterns of global integration in the region. Overall, the transformation from centrally planned to market economies in Central and Eastern Europe has produced a range of outcomes and models. Hungary and the Visegrad Four group occupy a distinct position in the global economy compared to further east countries like Russia and Ukraine, and other post-socialist emerging market economies like the Baltic states, Romania, and Slovenia (Bohle & Greskovits, 2012; Mykhenko, 2007; Nölke & Vliegenthart, 2009).

According to Nölke and Vliegenthart (2009, p. 648), coming to the region to exploit lower wages for their assembly operations, MNCs did not accept "factors such as high wages, high union density, comprehensive collective agreements, powerful worker representation or cumbersome procedures for layoffs." Drahokoupil and Myant (2016) followed this argument stating that the competitiveness of DMEs is not based on local innovations, but rather on imported technology, low-cost labor, and abundant raw materials. The success of these economic models is dependent on attractive institutional frameworks, such as stable legal environments for business, reliable employment relations, and strong international connections. Complex financial systems or the capacity for domestic innovation are not required, as these are provided by multinational companies. As a result, Central and Eastern European countries (CEECs) are dependent on innovation and financial systems that originate from other parts of the world (Drahokoupil & Myant, 2016).

Following this line of reasoning, some studies have shown that the MNCs' dependence on the favorable environment in the V4 countries is reciprocated, as they are also dependent on the MNCs (Pavlinek, 2016). Drahokoupil and Myant (2016) found that FDI increased the resilience of V4 countries during the Great Recession and that, although they were impacted to varying degrees, the manufacturing industry acted as a stabilizing factor, with Hungary being one of the most severely affected. However, they also pointed out that MNCs were not necessarily driving forces behind labor-market liberalization, as they were content with the low relative wage levels and preferred to avoid partisan politics. Domestic businesses, rather than MNCs, were found to carry more political weight and had a broader base for pressuring further reductions in employee protections. Therefore, Drahokoupil and Myant (2016) suggest that the receptiveness to neoliberal ideas was more due to the strengthening of the domestic high-income and business group than the direct influence of MNCs.

The following can be expected in regard to immigrant entrepreneurship in dependent market economies (DMEs), as demonstrated by the works of Pavlinek (2016) and Drahokoupil and Myant (2016). First, economic dependence does not necessarily lead to institutional dependence. Second, the high level of integration into global markets and proximity to advanced European markets attract immigrants and foreign business owners to start businesses in DMEs, as shown in the GEM organization report of 2021 where Hungary ranks in the middle among all countries monitored by the organization ("Research Summaries," 2022). Third, low wages and production costs can not only attract multinational corporations (MNCs), but also encourage entrepreneurship, including immigrant entrepreneurs, in DMEs. These assumptions require further examination of Hungarian migration policies and the emergence and characteristics of post-Soviet immigrant communities in Hungary. This is followed by an analysis of the dynamics of post-Soviet immigrant entrepreneurship in Hungary and the conclusion addresses the relationship between entrepreneurship and integration of post-Soviet immigrants in Hungary and provides its classification.

5.2 Transformation of the Hungarian Immigration Regime

In the second half of the twentieth century, Hungary was a member of the Socialist bloc and participated in interstate exchange programs. These programs allowed for the exchange of students and invitation of experts, but the stays were typically assumed to be temporary. Thus, similar to Austria by the late 1970s and Spain by the mid-1980s, Hungary (and other Socialist bloc states) did not have migration regulations. The countries of the Socialist bloc, including Hungary, opted for full employment economic policies and citizens of other bloc members working in Hungary had equal employment rights (Moricz, 2013).

However, after the collapse of the Socialist bloc, migration policies in Hungary changed. Initially, visa-free regimes remained between former socialist countries and were even extended to Western European countries. Before Hungary's EU accession, however, visas were introduced for citizens of non-EU countries, including the post-Soviet countries (except the Baltic states). As a result, the share of EU nationals among the migrant population in Hungary increased from 10 percent in the early 2000s to 21 percent in 2010 ("International Migration Outlook 2012," 2012). According to Moricz (2013), while the newcomer population in Hungary is better educated and more active in the labor force than the average, their employment is restricted. Third-country nationals (TCNs) can only be hired if they have a work permit or if they are long-term residents. The Labor Market Mobility Law, which came into effect in 2010, has improved this situation by granting equal access to self-employment.

In 2004, Hungary joined the EU but was unable to draft a successful immigration policy document like the Czech Republic and Slovakia did after their EU accession in the same year (Moricz, 2013). Hungary's post-EU-accession migration policies show a tension between its obligations as an EU member state and its perceived obligations to Hungarians in neighboring non-EU countries (Molodikova, 2014). In this institutional context, post-Soviet citizens were categorized as TCNs (Table 5.2).

Following the peak in immigration to Hungary in 2008 after joining the Schengen Agreement, the numbers started to decline due to the impact of the Great Recession. In 2010, the number of immigration decreased by 6 percent compared to the previous year and by 32 percent compared to 2009. The issuance of work permits also dropped by 13 percent in 2010 compared to the previous year, with two-thirds of them

Table 5.2 Development of Hungarian migration policy 1989–2022

Significant regulation/year	*Aim*	*Outcome*
1992 Visa-free regime with post-Socialist and EU countries	To increase mobility and accelerate integration with Western Europe	Liberalization of movement
2008 Schengen Agreement	Free movement of EU citizens	Immigration of highly educated EU citizens, and emigration of Hungarians to Austria, Germany, and the UK
2010–2011 Citizenship law	Simplified and preferential naturalization of Hungarians from neighboring countries and their families	In 2010, 6086 new Hungarian citizens; in January 2011–March 2012, 130,000 new Hungarian citizens (mainly from Romania)

Sources: OECD ("International Migration Outlook 2012," 2012), Moricz (2013), Molodikova (2014), Tepavcevic (2021) kormany.hu ("Honositas eddig 230 ezer allampolgarsagi kerelem erkezett," 2012)

being issued to immigrants from neighboring countries (Moricz, 2013). At the same time, the Great Recession led to an increase in the number of Hungarians leaving to work abroad, mainly to neighboring countries such as Austria's Burgenland, Germany, and the UK. Meanwhile, countries with large Hungarian minorities such as Romania, Ukraine, and Serbia sent the majority of migrants to Hungary (Moricz, 2013).

In 2010, the Hungarian government introduced a revised citizenship law that offered a streamlined and favored path to naturalization for Hungarians from neighboring countries. The law went into effect in 2011, but the decision for migrants to stay in Hungary was largely based on the presence or absence of their social networks, and no integration policy was established. As a result, only Hungarians from neighboring countries, and those immigrants who married Hungarians, had a chance to integrate into Hungarian society (Molodikova, 2014; Tepavcevic, 2021). Meanwhile, other TCNs faced lengthy and restrictive access to Hungarian citizenship. It takes them eight years to acquire citizenship after receiving a permanent residence permit, which requires at least three years of legal residency in the country. Thus, it typically takes up to eleven years for them to become citizens. Similarly, spouses of Hungarian citizens must prove three years of marriage and three years of residency in Hungary to be eligible to apply for citizenship (Moricz, 2013).

In 2010, the Hungarian government, led by Prime Minister Viktor Orban, introduced a policy of resident permits for foreign investors. A special immigration program was created for Chinese citizens who had to invest at least 250,000 Euro in Hungary in order to receive resident permits (Nagy et al., 2016). Similar programs were offered to other third-country nationals, including immigrants from post-Soviet non-EU countries. This policy reflects the relationship between Hungary's model of market economy and its immigration policy, which both aim to attract foreign investment. Financial resources are a main requirement for obtaining a resident permit, making the policy selective based on socioeconomic status and accepting wealthier third-country national immigrants. This policy encourages self-employment, entrepreneurship, and economic integration of immigrants in Hungary, independent of the country's labor market, while the macro-level economy relies on investments from large multinational corporations.

As an EU and Schengen member state with external EU borders, Hungary is a key transit country for irregular land migration to other EU countries. This has been a politically sensitive issue, particularly since the peak of the global migration crisis in 2015. In response, the Hungarian government, led by Viktor Orban, has taken a hardline stance against EU immigrant quotas and EU migration policy. To reduce irregular migration, the government has built border fences and enacted legal amendments. This has led to a decrease in asylum applications and irregular border crossings ("Hungary IOM," 2022). Additionally, Orban has made migration and sovereignty a priority in his political agenda and has launched a permanent anti-immigrant campaign, including the construction of a border fence on Hungary's southern border (Biro-Nagy, 2021). According to Eurostat (2021), in 2021 only 2 percent of Hungary's population were immigrants, with 75,719 or 1 percent being citizens of other EU countries, and 118,400 or another 1 percent being third-country nationals. The Hungarian immigration regime has three main features. First, it supports the free movement within the EU and fully adheres to Schengen laws. Second, it implements a strict and unsupportive policy toward third-country nationals of non-Hungarian origin; and third, it clearly supports the immigration of ethnic Hungarians from neighboring countries and their families, which results in a *jus sanguinis* immigration regime that extends to families.

5.3 Soviet and Post-Soviet Immigration and Communities in Hungary: Waves, Motives, and Paths

During the twentieth century, migration from former Soviet republics to Hungary took place through four channels. The first was the presence of 60,000 southern Soviet troops located in various cities across Hungary, with the largest communities residing in Budapest, Paks, and Debrecen. They established hospitals, schools, clubs, and shops, where the officers' spouses worked to support their own needs for education and income (Molodikova, 2014). The second channel was through marriage, with most Hungarians who studied in the FSU marrying Soviet citizens during their studies and then returning to Hungary with their spouse after graduation. Intergovernmental agreements between socialist bloc countries allowed Soviet citizens in Hungary access to the labor market. The third channel was through exchange programs for students, which recognized education degrees and allowed FSU citizens in Hungary to integrate into the local society through employment. The fourth channel was through the presence of Soviet companies' representative offices in Hungary: Western European and North American migration studies typically categorize these migrants as expatriates or "expats," or as migrant professionals (Meier, 2015).

In the aftermath of the collapse of the Socialist bloc, many Soviet immigrants to Hungary, including those who came through marriage, exchange programs, and work for Soviet companies, remained in the country because they lacked perspectives in their home countries. This led to the formation of the first Russian-speaking immigrant community in Hungary. Despite facing similar economic difficulties as the local Hungarians due to shrinking job market and high unemployment, these unintentional post-Soviet immigrants did not feel excluded from Hungarian society (Tepavcevic, 2021). While they faced administrative and social challenges as citizens of a former occupying nation, these post-Soviet immigrants also experienced economic difficulties and discrimination. As one of them recalled in one of private conversations, "during the sport class in the school we had a task to take each other's hands to dance, but my classmates refused to take my hand because I came from the Soviet Union" (personal communication, October 2012). Facing social exclusion, they formed both informal associations and small businesses responding to the demands of the emerging post-Soviet immigrant community, thus representing common-culture-based entrepreneurship. At the same time, the collapse of the Soviet Union resulted in a wave of immigration to Hungary, with many former Soviet citizens staying in the country. According to one of the former Hungarian diplomats, in the early 1990s, many criminal post-Soviet groups came to Hungary for money-laundering and safety reasons. Creating temporary employment for their compatriots who already resided in Hungary (personal communication, May 2020), by the end of the 1990s most of them moved to Western Europe and the Czech Republic in search for wealthier markets (Tepavcevic, 2017).

Driven by the geographical expansion of MNCs, in the early 2000s, highly skilled post-Soviet labor migrants started to immigrate to Hungary, usually as employees of MNCs. In the same period, Hungary also attracted post-Soviet small-to-mid-scale businesspersons. These immigrant groups also founded some formal associations, including the Council of Compatriots, the Russian Theatre, and the Ukrainian school. Several thematic Russian-language Facebook groups also emerged in Hungary over the last decade. Responding to the growing post-Soviet immigrant community, in 2016, Hungary's first state TV channel M1 launched news broadcasts in various foreign languages, including Russian. This contrasts with the situation in Austria and Spain, where despite larger post-Soviet immigrant populations and more developed integration policies, Russian-language media has only appeared in the form of immigrant-owned businesses.

Over the last three decades, the number of post-Soviet immigrant communities in Hungary has ranged between 10,000 and 15,000, and it is constantly evolving. The last two waves of post-Soviet immigration to Hungary were due to the violent conflict in Ukraine. In 2014, when the conflict began, many Russian, Ukrainian, and Belarussian professionals and business owners immigrated to Hungary. The current wave of post-Soviet migration to Hungary is a result of the ongoing Russian government's invasion of Ukraine, and it is unclear how many Ukrainian refugees, Russian emigrants, and asylum seekers will ultimately settle in Hungary.

5.4 Classification of Post-Soviet Entrepreneurship in Hungary

As discussed in previous chapters, the timing of immigration has influenced the type and form of post-Soviet immigrant entrepreneurship in Austria and Spain. The same holds true for post-Soviet immigration in Hungary. Further classification of post-Soviet entrepreneurship in

Hungary combines the place in host country's market reflected in the size and sector of entrepreneurship, with the relation of entrepreneurship to the post-Soviet immigrant community, and the role of entrepreneurship in immigrants' integration in a host country. Some Soviet migrants who arrived in the late 1980s utilized their embeddedness in the Hungarian society and capitalized on the political and economic changes in Hungary to establish their own businesses. One such business is *Detki* (Kids), a successful producer of biscuits under a well-known Hungarian brand. Its founder and co-owner, Olga Pavlova, acquired and refurbished a production site in Halmaugra, northeast of Budapest, in 1989. Today, *Detki* is recognized as one of the most prominent mid-sized food companies in Hungary and a popular brand of biscuits. According to an associate of the owner, "*Detki* is a Hungarian company, it employs Hungarians, and functions as an integral part of the Hungarian economy with no reliance on the Russian-speaking community" (personal communication, November 2018). Therefore, apart from being founded by a former Soviet citizen and having a Russian-named brand, *Detki* does not differ from any other Hungarian food production business, providing the owner with complete socioeconomic integration in Hungary. These features combined place *Detki* into a distinct—integrative—type of immigrant entrepreneurship.

Rossiyskiy Kuryer (The Russian Courier), a Russian language journal founded by a journalist couple in the late 1980s, served as an early platform for post-Soviet immigrants in Hungary (Tepavcevic, 2017). As one of the most successful businesses started by post-Soviet immigrants, the journal provided a connection between former compatriots and also served as an advertisement venue for their emerging businesses. As mobility between Hungary and Austria and other EU member states increased in the 2000s, the journal expanded its coverage to include political and social life in Austria, with a focus on the local post-Soviet immigrant community. However, its coverage of Austria proved less successful than its original focus on Hungary due to higher living costs in Austria and competition from established local media (personal communication, May 2017). With digitalization, the journal continued its work in Hungary and expanded its reach to include wealthy post-Soviet communities in France, where the family behind the journal relocated (personal communication, December 2019). Today, the Russian Courier can be considered a multinational small business that plays a role in connecting post-Soviet immigrants across the EU.

In the early 1990s, post-Soviet migration in Hungary also created opportunities for trade, retail, and logistics businesses. Former Soviet procurement services organized the first retail shops selling food products from various ethnic cuisines from the former Soviet republics, with the largest being the food-products chain *Arbat*. Other businesses profited by offering transport and logistics services (personal communication, March 2015). These companies have fluctuated in size and activity depending on the size of the post-Soviet immigrant community in Hungary and global economic trends. *Arbat*, for example, had eleven shops across Hungary and a restaurant in the early 2000s. However, after the global economic crisis, only two shops remain operating in downtown Budapest. *Arbat* still relies on post-Soviet networks in Germany and Hungary for product supply and employs FSU immigrants, serving customers that are a mix of Hungarians, post-Soviets, EU citizens, and tourists. *Smak* (Taste), another similar retail shop in downtown Budapest, specializes in online trade and delivery and caters primarily to the post-Soviet immigrant community in Hungary (personal communication, December 2019). As a result, these retail businesses ranged in type of immigrant entrepreneurship between grassroots and *corporants*. At the end of 2022, both *Arbat* and *Smak* resembled mostly common-culture-based grassroots immigrant entrepreneurship seen in Austria and Spain in terms of their legal forms and size.

Similarly, during the 1990s transformations in Hungary, a group of Soviet companies utilized their networks to trade in used Soviet and Eastern European vehicles and spare parts. However, as Western European direct investment rose in the Hungarian automotive industry, these businesses either pivoted to trading used European vehicles and parts or went out of business, with their owners transitioning to other industries (Tepavcevic, 2017). This shift in the economy led to an increased demand for language learning, particularly in Hungarian and Russian, among the post-Soviet immigrant community in Hungary. This demand resulted in the creation of *Alfavit* (Alphabet), a non-profit language school founded by Rita Hasanova, who formerly acted as a representative of one of the Soviet companies in Hungary. In addition to language classes, *Alfavit* also offers music and arts programs and co-hosts cultural events and summer camps for post-Soviet immigrant children in Hungary and across the EU, in partnership with the Russian Theater and Councils of Compatriots. Before the COVID-19 pandemic, the school organized summer camps in Hungary and other EU countries in collaboration with language schools and Councils of Compatriots (personal communication, December 2017).

As a result, *Alfavit* acts as a connector for post-Soviet immigrant communities in Hungary and throughout the EU, playing a crucial role in unifying these communities. Similar to the founders of the *New Viennese Journal* in Austria and Russian-Inn-Spain journal in Spain, and along with founders of Russian Courier in Hungary, the founder of *Alfavit* acts as an informal leader of the post-Soviet immigrant community in Hungary. Significant fact is that they all are female immigrant entrepreneurs. The durability of their businesses affirms their success and serves as inspiring examples of connector-type immigrant entrepreneurship.

The Rakhimkulov family has been a well-known example of post-Soviet immigrant entrepreneurship. Megdet Rakhimkulov came to Hungary in 1994 as the official representative of Gazprom Corporation and the chair of the Hungarian-Russian gas supply joint venture, Panrusgaz. Along with his role at Panrusgaz, Rakhimkulov and his sons owned and ran various businesses through their Hungarian company, Kafijat, with the key asset being AEB Bank, later acquired by Gazprombank. This bank served Russian companies involved in investment projects in Hungary, including MDM Group, Zenit Bank, and Uralsib (Orban, 2008; Weiner, 2015). Rakhimkulov became one of the wealthiest residents of Hungary, and AEB had corporate clients such as Zalakeramia, Antenna, Hungarian Gas Trade, MVM, Hungarian Business Telecom, Borsodchem, Mol, and Magyar Telekom (Weiner, 2015).

Due to AEB's frequent dealings with Russian state-owned companies and banks, the Rakhimkulovs were seen as conduits of Russian state interests in Hungary. With their businesses closely tied to the FDI of Russian state companies, this form of immigrant entrepreneurship can be classified as FDI-generated. The Rakhimkulovs serve as a vivid illustration of expats becoming immigrant entrepreneurs. At the same time, the Rakhimkulovs have maintained a certain degree of distance from the majority of the post-Soviet immigrant community in the country (as confirmed through personal communication with two associates in September 2019). Megdet Rakhimkulov retired and returned to Russia in 2013 after the Great Recession, while most of his family members stayed in Hungary. One of the family members, Ruslan Rakhimkulov, runs an entertainment company named *Magyar Virtuozok* (Hungarian Virtuosos) in Hungary (Tepavcevic, 2017). The company, while capitalizing on the owner's connections to Russia, is fully integrated into the Hungarian entertainment industry and hosts theater performances and concerts featuring renowned artists from around the world, including Russia. Therefore, unlike Kafijat,

Hungarian Virtuosos can be classified as integrative type of immigrant entrepreneurship, while its founder, Ruslan Rakhimkulov remains one of the wealthiest residents of Hungary.

Reax Invest is also one of the prominent players in the Hungarian development and construction sector founded by post-Soviet immigrants. With its roots dating back to 1997, Reax has grown into one of the largest real estate developers in the country, having built and sold over 3000 apartments primarily in Budapest and its surrounding areas ("Reax," 1997–2022). The company's real estate development team comprises both Ukrainian and Hungarian employees, with Hungarian staff providing all client services, and it caters to both the Hungarian market and, to a lesser extent, foreign clients (personal communication, October 2019). However, unlike its Austrian counterpart, Luxury Immobilien, Reax focuses more on the mass market and offers fewer luxury options. Along with *Detki* and Hungarian Virtuosos, Reax embodies the integrative form of immigrant entrepreneurship in Hungary, being deeply embedded in the Hungarian real estate development industry.

The businesses established by the second wave of post-Soviet immigrants in Hungary were varied. In the early 2000s, changes in Hungary's international status and the EU's increasingly strict visa regimes made it more difficult for citizens of post-Soviet countries to enter Hungary. However, an improving economic situation in these countries, coupled with growing multinational corporation activity across Hungary, drew professionals from all over the world, including post-Soviet countries. As a result, entrepreneurship became part of many post-Soviet immigration plans to Hungary and the EU. Many Russian and Ukrainian students who came to study in Hungarian universities started businesses while still in school or shortly after graduation. One such company was 1000 Roads, a travel agency that soon expanded into the hospitality sector (online communication, November 2021). Owning offices and hotels in Budapest and co-owning a hotel in the famous Hungarian resort of Heviz and an office in Hajduszobloszlo (Tepavcevic, 2017), the company employed post-Soviet immigrants in Hungary, consolidating them into a coherent immigrant community. Therefore, similar to Alegria in Spain, 1000 Roads in Hungary resembles corporant-type immigrant entrepreneurship. Operating both in Hungary and, more recently, in Russia, 1000 Roads is an example of a typical transnational immigrant business, as defined by Nazareno et al. (2018).

The post-Soviet immigrant community in Hungary demonstrated a diverse range of entrepreneurial ventures between 2000 and 2011, including personal trainers in various fields, a shoe production and retail chain, and tourist guides. For example, Anna Zaboeva, a Russian artist and shoe designer, created a unique business by repurposing used clothes, carpets, and accessories to make new shoes (Tepavcevic, 2017). She sold her shoes in her own retail stores in Budapest, Bratislava, and Ljubljana and her business was a prime example of grassroots-level immigrant entrepreneurship that was also truly European in scale.

The Great Recession resulted in low real estate costs in Hungary, attracting foreign investors and companies, primarily from Russia. These companies registered in Hungary and operated as small and medium-sized businesses, employing citizens of Hungary and Ukraine. The small-scale investor established the company in order to obtain permanent residency in Hungary through the company's business activities.

> Coming from then extremely expensive and overcrowded Moscow, Budapest seemed as the quiet oasis. Food, clothes, and real estate—was considerably cheaper than in Moscow. I realized that even with my relatively small savings earned during my work in Moscow I could start a business in Hungary, so recognizing a demand, I established a real estate renovation company. The company's activity also provided me with the basis for receiving my permanent residence in Hungary after my graduation. (Personal communication, October 2018)

Therefore, this micro company operating in Hungary is a representative of the increasing trend of post-Soviet immigrant entrepreneurship in the country. It operates alongside larger companies such as *Detki*, Hungarian Virtuosos, and Reax Invest encompassing an integrative type of immigrant entrepreneurship.

The COVID-19 pandemic has seen a new wave of post-Soviet immigration in Hungary, especially in the IT sector. IT Kitchen, a software development company originally founded in Russia, is one such example. With patents registered in the USA and employees from various post-Soviet countries, the company relocated to Hungary due to unfavorable conditions for SMEs in Russia, including a lack of political representation of their interests and difficulties participating in state procurement tenders. Faced with growing political and economic pressures in Russia, the founders and managers of a booming IT business sought a new location for their company.

> After exploring options all across Europe and Asia, we found a more favorable environment for credit and growth in Hungary. While the costs of immigration, living, and business operations are lower in Hungary compared to the US, UK, and Western Europe, the quality of business services is also lower. (Personal communication, November 2022)

However, the company prioritizes keeping their team of developers together and continues to operate their business, serving clients in the EU and beyond, after registering the company in Hungary. The founders of IT Kitchen offered relocation to Hungary to all their employees from Russia. Many accepted and relocated as soon as their business visas and work permits were processed. This move represents both a way to escape unfavorable conditions for SMEs in Russia and seek improved living conditions and legal immigration.

> When Russia's army invaded Ukraine, we invited our colleagues from Ukraine to join us in Hungary, but most of them are male between the ages of eighteen and sixty and due to martial law travel ban, they are not allowed to leave the country. (Personal communication, November 2022)

Aside from the IT sector, many post-Soviet immigrants in Hungary who previously worked in the tourism industry lost their jobs during and after the COVID-19 pandemic. Some started their own small businesses in sectors like beauty and sports. Previously, there was no entrepreneurship in Hungary related to legal services, but after the pandemic, one law office emerged that specializes in real estate purchases and immigration questions, mainly for Russian and Ukrainian citizens (personal communication, October 2022).

5.5 Conclusions: The Role of Entrepreneurship in Integration of Post-Soviet Immigrants in Hungary

The collapse of both their home country and Hungary's systems resulted in the formation of a group of unintentional post-Soviet immigrants in Hungary who turned to entrepreneurship as a means of survival. This group primarily operates in sectors they were previously employed in, such as retail, logistics, media, and tourism. Their entrepreneurship turned them from temporary migrant professionals into permanent immigrant entrepreneurs. In turn, this entrepreneurship to some extend reflects the cultural enclave theory of immigrant entrepreneurship, where immigrants create businesses in their familiar cultural and industry niches (Light, 1984; Portes & Wilson, 1980; Tepavcevic, 2021).

Therefore, during and after the fall of the Soviet bloc and the transformation of Hungary into a democratic and market-based economy, post-Soviet immigrant entrepreneurship was driven primarily by the necessity created by the economic changes, as well as negative attitudes toward citizens of the former occupier of Hungary. As a result, most post-Soviet entrepreneurship took the form of common-culture-based enclaves in logistics, retail, and media and was classified as grassroots immigrant entrepreneurship. This finding aligns with early theories of immigrant entrepreneurship developed in the USA, which suggest that limited access to the host country's labor market and demand from the immigrant community drive the creation of economies where supply, demand, and social capital come from the immigrant community (Kontos, 2003; Portes, 1997). This period also saw the emergence of other post-Soviet-founded companies, including the still-existing biscuit factory *Detki*, which represents low-tech entrepreneurship and, as such, is a typical example of DME entrepreneurship according to Dilli et al. (2018). In terms of its role in immigrant integration, this company is classified as integrative, as its operations are fully integrated into the Hungarian food industry. The wave of post-Soviet immigration to Hungary during the 1990s helped these businesses to grow and expand.

As this chapter shows, post-Soviet immigrants in later waves of migration to Hungary faced more structural challenges compared to earlier waves, including tighter visa regulations and limited access to the labor market. However, a significant number of these second-wave post-Soviet immigrants arrived in Hungary in the 2000s as students or employees of multinational corporations. These MNCs played a crucial role in transforming Hungary's economy into a market-oriented one, and as a result, these post-Soviet immigrants mainly integrated into international immigrant or expat communities. For many of these immigrants, entrepreneurship became a way to attain permanent residency and a primary source of income, similar to their former compatriots who emigrated to Austria and Spain around the same time. For example, entrepreneurship provided a path to legal integration for those who came as students. Overall, as

Table 5.3 Types, forms, and sectors of post-Soviet immigrant entrepreneurship in Hungary

Sectors and forms of post-Soviet entrepreneurship in Hungary	*Type of immigrant entrepreneurship*
Food production, entertainment, real estate development and renovation micro, SME, and large companies	Integrative immigrant entrepreneurship
Retail, logistics, construction, retail shops, beauty services	Grassroots common-culture-based and transnational immigrant entrepreneurship
Media, education centers, legal and medical services	Connectors between the Hungarians, Hungary-based, and EU post-Soviet immigrant communities
Hospitality firms—hotels and restaurants	*Corporants* immigrant entrepreneurship
IT Companies	International Re-locators immigrant entrepreneur
Multisector large business	FDI-generated immigrant entrepreneurship

Table 5.3 shows, the types and forms of post-Soviet immigrant entrepreneurship in Hungary have evolved over time, from common-culture-based food production in the 1990s to currently growing IT services, and remain diverse.

The study partially supports the theory on the impact of the time of arrival on post-Soviet entrepreneurship, as proposed, for example, by Ryazantsev et al. (2018). However, it also highlights the importance of historical-geographical contexts that Jessop (2011) labeled "spacio-temporal fixies." The findings also demonstrate that both the home and host countries' international positions influence immigrant entrepreneurship, which is similar to the argument proposed in relation to FDI by Tepavcevic (2018). The Hungarian economic model, which has relied on FDI for economic development, has also attracted immigrant entrepreneurs for similar reasons as multinational corporations: access to the European Union market, relatively low operational costs, and a relatively inexpensive labor force.

References

Biro-Nagy, A. (2021). Orbán's Political Jackpot: Migration and the Hungarian Electorate. *Journal of Ethnic and Migration Studies, 48*(2), 405–424.

Bohle, D., & Greskovits, B. (2012). *Capitalist Diversity on Europe's Periphery.* Cornell University Press.

Csaba, L. (2007). *The New Political Economy of Emerging Europe*. Akademiai Kiado.
Dilli, S., Elert, N., & Herrmann, A. (2018). Varieties of Entrepreneurship: Exploring the Institutional Foundations of Different Entrepreneurship Types through 'Varieties-of-Capitalism' Arguments. *Small Business Economics, 51*(2), 293–320.
Drahokoupil, J., & Myant, M. (2016). Dependent Capitalism and Employment Relations in East Central Europe. In *Social Transformations in Central and Eastern Europe: Europeanization and Beyond* (pp. 42–59). Routledge.
Eurostat (2021). https://ec.europa.eu/eurostat/statistics-explained/index.php?title=Migration_and_migrant_population_statistics
Eurostat, 2022 Real GDP per capita. (2022). https://ec.europa.eu. Retrieved from https://ec.europa.eu/eurostat/databrowser/view/tessi190/default/table?lang=en
Feldmann, M. (2019). Global Varieties of Capitalism. *World Politics, 71*(1), 162–196.
Honositas eddig 230 ezer allampolgarsagi kerelem erkezett. (2012, March 14).
Hungary IOM. (2022). https://hungary.iom.int/
International Migration Outlook 2012. (2012).
Jessop, B. (2011). Rethinking the Diversity and Variability of Capitalism: On Variegated Capitalism in the World Market. In *Capitalist Diversity and Diversity within Capitalism* (pp. 233–261). Routledge.
King, L. P. (2007). Central European Capitalism in Comparative Perspective. In *Beyond Varieties of Capitalism: Conflict, Contradiction and Complementarities in the European Economy* (pp. 307–327). Oxford University Press.
Kontos, M. (2003). Self-employment Policies and Migrants' Entrepreneurship in Germany. *Entrepreneurship and Regional Development, 15*(2), 119–135.
Light, I. (1984). Immigrant and Ethnic Enterprise in North America. *Ethnic and Racial Studies, 7*(2), 195–216.
Meier, L. (Ed.). (2015). *Migrant Professionals in the City. Local Encounters, Identities and Inequalities*. Routledge.
Molodikova, I. (2014). Russian Policy toward Compatriots: Diversities and Contradictions of Its Implementation. In *Post-Soviet Diasporas: Identities, Linkages, and Transformation* (pp. 20–21). Carleton.
Moricz, I. (Producer). (2013). An Overview of the Migration Policies and Trends—Hungary. https://migrationonline.cz
Myant, M., & Drahokoupil, J. (2011). *Transition Economies: Political Economy in Russia, Eastern Europe, and Central Asia*. John Wiley and Sons Inc.
Mykhenko, V. (2007). Strengths and Weaknesses of 'Weak' Coordination: Economic Institutions, Revealed Comparative Advantages, and Socio-Economic Performance of Mixed Market Economies in Poland and Ukraine. In *Beyond Varieties of Capitalism: Conflict, Contradictions, and Complementarities in the European Economy* (Chap. 13). Oxford University Press.

Nagy, B., Ligeti, M., & Martin, J. P. (2016). *In Whose Interest?: Shadows Over the Hungarian Residency Bond Program.*

Nazareno, J., Zhou, M., & You, T. (2018). Global Dynamics of Immigrant Entrepreneurship. Changing Trends, Ethnonational Variations, and Reconceptualizations. *International Journal of Entrepreneurial Behavior & Research.* https://doi.org/10.1108/IJEBR-03-2018-0141

Nölke, A., & Vliegenthart, A. (2009). Enlarging the Varieties of Capitalism: The Emergence of Dependent Market Economies in East Central Europe. *World Politics, 61*(4), 670–702.

Orban, A. (2008). *Power, Energy, and the New Russian Imperialism.* Praeger Security International.

Pavlinek, P. (2016). Whose Success? The State-Foreign Capital Nexus and the Development of the Automotive Industry in Slovakia. *European Urban and Regional Studies, 23*(4), 571–593.

Portes, A. (1997). *Globalization from Below: The Rise of Transnational Communities.* Princeton University.

Portes, A., & Wilson, K. L. (1980). Immigrant Enclaves: An Analysis of the Labor Market Experiences of Cubans in Miami. *The American Journal of Sociology, 86*, 295–319.

Reax. (1997–2022). https://reax.hu/

Research Summaries. (2022).

Ryazantsev, S., Pismennaya, E., Lukyantsev, A., Sivoplyasova, S., & Khramova, M. (2018). Modern Emigration from Russia and Formation of Russian-Speaking Communities Abroad (In Russian). *World Economy and International Relations, 62*(6), 93–107.

Streeck, W., & Thelen, K. (2005). *Beyond Continuity: Institute of Advanced Political Economies.* Oxford University Press.

Tepavcevic, S. (2017). Immigrant Entrepreneurship in the Post-Socialist Countries of the European Union: Motives and Patterns of Entrepreneurship of Post-Soviet Immigrants in Hungary. *Migration and Ethnic Themes, 1*, 65–92.

Tepavcevic, S. (2018). In the Bear's Shadow? Russia's International Image and Its Influence on Investments of Russian Companies in Post-Socialist Europe. *Journal of East-West Business, 24*(2), 108–137.

Tepavcevic, S. (2021). Changing Geography, Retaining the Mentality: Social and Economic Integration of Post-Soviet Immigrants in Austria and Hungary. *Review of Economic Theory and Policy, 3*, 137–154.

Weiner, C. (2015). Tracking Russian FDI in Hungary. *East European Studies*, (6), 120–168. http://real.mtak.hu/34126/1/Weiner_Tracking....pdf

PART III

CHAPTER 6

Varieties of EU Economic Models, Immigration Regimes, and Post-Soviet Immigrant Entrepreneurship

Abstract This chapter examines the similarities and differences in post-Soviet immigrant entrepreneurship by analyzing the economic models, immigration regimes, size, and nature of post-Soviet immigrant communities and the forms of their entrepreneurship. The results show that the economic models and immigration regimes of different countries are interdependent and determine the diverse types of post-Soviet immigrant entrepreneurship. By comparing the immigration regimes in Austria, Spain, and Hungary, the chapter reveals that the regime in Hungary is a new subtype of the broader EU immigration regime and is integrated with Hungary's market economy model, referred to as the Extra-Union-Plus immigration regime.

Keywords Economic models • Immigration regimes • Entrepreneurship typology • Immigrant communities • Post-Soviet migrants

S. Tepavcevic, *Diversity of Migrant Entrepreneurship in Varieties of European Capitalism*,
https://doi.org/10.1007/978-3-031-31097-3_6

6.1 Economic Development, VoC Economic Models, and Their Need in Immigrant Labor Force

The analysis of post-Soviet immigrant entrepreneurship in Austria, Hungary, and Spain displays the relevance of national contexts in the emergence of their immigration regimes, various immigrant communities, and forms of immigrant entrepreneurships. Austria became one of the most developed countries in Europe by the mid-1960s due to rapid post-war modernization, geographic location, and military neutrality. These factors, combined with the system of coordinated industrial relations persistent since the industrialization, resulted in a coordinated market economy (CME) model characterized by a social safety net, incremental innovation, development based on coordination and cooperation between similar businesses, and high taxes aimed at sustaining the public services, high employment and salaries, and high levels of social equality. Temporary foreign labor was used to fill production gaps and low-skilled positions. As a result, even as a member of the EU, EMU, and Schengen, Austria's CME model appears relatively stable and considerably resilient to various global shocks.

In contrast, political and economic modernization in Spain took place only in the mid-1970s, resulting in rapid economic growth averaging around 3.5 percent annually, which is almost twice lower than Austria's average annual growth in the late 1950s. The growth in Spain was not evenly distributed across industries and geography. In addition to existing agriculture, fishing, and tourism that thrived due to the favorable geography and climate, reforms boosted construction and real estate. Other industries such as automotive, textile, and fashion gradually became competitive on the global market by the late 1990s and early 2000s when Spain was already a member of the EU. This emergence of the mixed market economy (MME) model in Spain was closely tied to EU membership, and long-term low-skilled immigrant labor was required to sustain increased production and consumption. Spanish immigration policy prioritized immigrants from former Spanish colonies and citizens of other EU member states in integration through the labor market by default.

Hungary underwent political and economic reforms that modernized its economy fifteen years after Spain. Its average annual economic growth between 1990 and 2000 was slightly above 4 percent, between Austria and Spain. Hungary's cheap, skilled labor force and existing industrial infrastructure, combined with proximity to Western Europe, attracted

Table 6.1 Comparison of Real GDP per capita and Gini Coefficient in Austria, Spain, and Hungary

Country	*Year*	*2010*	*2015*	*2020*
Austria	Real GDP per capita in Euro per capita	35,398	36,148	35,480
	Gini Coefficient (0 = total equality, 1 = total inequality)	28.3	27.2	27.8
Spain	Real GDP per capita in Euro per capita	23,040	23,090	22,210
	Gini Coefficient (0 = total equality, 1 = total inequality)	32.5	34.6	32.1
Hungary	Real GDP per capita in Euro per capita	9988	11,228	12,730
	Gini Coefficient (0 = total equality, 1 = total inequality)	24.1	28.2	28.8

Source: Eurostat ("Eurostat, 2022 Real GDP per capita," 2022)

MNCs and FDI, primarily in the automotive and high-tech manufacturing sectors. MNCs also capitalized on lower operational costs compared to nearby Austria and Germany, and Hungary's EU and Schengen memberships provided institutional stability (Table 6.1).

Overall, the analysis of varieties of European economic models reveals that there are three key factors influencing the emergence of these models: the first is the time of their political and economic modernization, the second is their geographical positions, and the third is their colonial histories. International political position of each of these countries also plays an equally important role in the emergence and functioning of the system. These findings reflect Jessop's (2011) term "spacio-temporal fixies" proving Streeck and Thelen's (2005) thesis about the constancy of institutional change, but also rejecting their argument about the inevitability of the liberalization process.

6.2 Varieties of Immigration Regimes, or VoIR: Comparing Immigration Regimes in Austria, Spain, and Hungary

The analysis of post-Soviet immigrant entrepreneurship in the three national contexts demonstrated their relevance in emergence of immigration regimes, various immigrant communities, and varieties of immigrant entrepreneurships. In contrast to economic modernization, the immigration regimes of Austria, Spain, and Hungary experienced similar significant changes in the early 1990s. This timing was due to the collapse of the Socialist bloc that had a global impact, particularly in Europe. Another similarity is that each country's immigration regime was shaped by its emerging economic model. The analysis in Chap. 3 suggests that the Austrian immigration regime is an integral part of the country's coordinated economic model. The coordination between business and non-market actors in Austria leaves immigrants marginalized, whether on the local level or in the national and global economies. This affects new arrivals, whose numbers have increased with Austria's economic growth. Over time, recognition of workers who remained in Austria and brought their families led to reforms in integration policies and regulations toward a *jus soli* principle. However, much of the reform in the Austrian immigration regime was driven by EU immigration regulations. As a result, the immigration regime has evolved from a highly restrictive jus sanguinis—based on ethnic and cultural origins—to a similarly restrictive jus soli based on length of stay and knowledge of the local language (German). Despite being one of the most advanced economies, the institutional system in Austria reinforces its traditional restrictions toward immigrants and outsiders, as categorized by Boucher and Gest (2018) as the Intra-Union subtype. This highlights the close relationship between the CME VoC economic model and the Intra-Union immigration regime.

According to the analysis in Chap. 4, the Spanish immigration regime has undergone gradual reforms over time. Prior to the 1990s, Spain was traditionally an emigration country and had not considered immigration and integration regulations. However, during a period of rapid economic growth, the government realized that Spanish low-skilled workers were not enough to meet the labor force requirements, leading to a need for immigration policies. Unlike Austria, Spain had a form of *jus soli* regulation in place even before joining the Schengen agreement, which granted citizenship to immigrants who legally resided in Spain for over ten years. As a result, the Spanish immigration regime transformed from highly restrictive in the 1990s and 2000s to semi-neoliberal for citizens of other EU countries and former Spanish colonies at the beginning of 2022. Despite the shift toward a more liberal regime, the Spanish immigration policies still remain moderately restrictive toward third-country nationals (TCNs). In this sense, the results of the analysis demonstrate a link between Spain's MME and the Extra-Union subtype of immigration regime, as defined by Boucher and Gest (2018).

The Hungarian immigration regime is characterized by its openness to Hungarians from the neighboring countries, citizens of other EU countries, and by its restrictiveness toward low-skilled labor. This approach is due to the government's concern over competition with the local workforce, as well as the preference of multinational corporations to hire and relocate professionals from other countries. As a result, Hungary's immigration regime has evolved as an extended form of the *jus sanguinis* principle, offering preferential treatment to Hungarians from neighboring countries and their descendants, as well as foreign family members of Hungarians. However, the country's dependence on foreign investment has influenced its "Eastern Openness" policy since 2012, aimed at balancing increased dependence on FDI from the EU. This policy has resulted in a small-scale investment-based residency program, attracting relatively wealthy third-country nationals, mainly from China and the former Soviet Union.

The Hungarian immigration regime shares similarities with both the Spanish Extra-Union regime and the Intra-European subtype of the pan-EU "Free Movement" immigration regime as defined by Boucher and Gest (2018). Despite being restrictive to low-skilled labor force, it remains relatively open and liberal toward foreign investors, granting residence permits to TCNs in return for small-scale investments sufficient to sustain immigrants' residence in Hungary. This reveals the emergence of the immigration regime related to Hungary's dependence on FDI and its "Eastern Openness" policy, aimed at counterbalancing the increased dependence on EU FDI. The investment-based residency program, combined with the *jus sanguinis* principle that covers Hungarians from non-EU members, gives the Hungarian immigration regime characteristics of both the Spanish Extra-Union regime and the Intra-European subtype of the pan-EU "Free Movement" immigration regime. As such, the Hungarian immigration regime can be conceptualized as an Extra-Union-Plus immigration regime subtype.

6.3 Comparing Post-Soviet Immigration and Communities in Austria, Spain, and Hungary

Among the three EU countries analyzed regarding post-Soviet immigration, Hungary is an exception due to its former membership in the Socialist bloc. It is due to this membership that the existence of immigrants and their communities from the FSU was made possible prior to radical transformations of the 1990s. These communities to some extent resembled Northern American and Western European expatriates when it comes to their functioning. Additionally, Hungary was the only country out of the three that were analyzed which shared a border with the former Soviet Union. It also represents the only country with an immigration regime representative of both wealthy and middle-class post-Soviet immigrants. Despite Hungary's advantages over Austria and Spain as a potential immigrant destination for post-Soviet citizens, it is host to the smallest immigration community, as shown in Table 6.2.

The number and size of post-Soviet immigrant communities in Austria, Spain, and Hungary reflect the levels of socioeconomic development and immigration policies of the respective countries. The more developed a country, the stricter its immigration policies tend to be, as seen in Austria's restrictions on immigration for both high-skilled and low-skilled post-Soviet immigrants. This highly restrictive immigration regime emerged as CME's by-product, integrating high-skilled young post-Soviet professionals into the labor market and pushing newcomers either to global markets or toward the post-Soviet culture-based enclave in Austria regardless of their qualifications. On the other hand, Spain's fragility of low-production-led economic growth has led to some liberalization of immigration policies for low-skilled workers, but restrictions in access to labor market remain for high-skilled and wealthy third-countries nationals, including post-Soviet immigrants. Such restrictions and the consequent

Table 6.2 Post-Soviet immigrant communities in Austria, Spain, and Hungary

Country	*Austria*[a]	*Spain*[b]	*Hungary*[c]
Total population	8,979,894	47,555,830	9,600,192
Immigrant population	1,587,251 (17%)	5,400,000 (15.23%)	220,000 (2%)
Post-Soviet immigrants	46,000 (33,895 Russians and 12,668 Ukrainians)	230,000 (79,485 Russians and 150,000 Ukrainians)	15,000 (10,000 Russians, 4500 Ukrainians, 500 others)

[a]Statistics Austria, Migration ("Statistics Austria—migration," 2021–2022)
[b]The Olive Press (2022)
[c]European Commission (2021)

marginalization in some cases imply some forms of destructive entrepreneurship (Sauka, 2008) in Austria's CME and generate some levels of gray economy in Spain's MME. Data shows that post-Soviet immigrants take advantage of the EU-Free-Movement policy and frequently move from one EU member state to another in search of better living conditions, business opportunities, or lower costs of living. This highlights the importance of the EU immigration regime for post-Soviet immigrants once they have overcome immigration barriers.

6.4 Comparing Post-Soviet Immigrant Entrepreneurship in Austria, Spain, and Hungary

The relationship between the time of modernization, socioeconomic development, and restrictiveness of immigration regimes also affects post-Soviet immigrant entrepreneurship in Austria, Spain, and Hungary. Economic development and immigration policies to varying degrees drive post-Soviet immigrants toward entrepreneurship. Findings in Austria indicate that the technical innovativeness found across CMEs by Dilli et al. (2018) does not apply to post-Soviet immigrant entrepreneurship in Austria; as local industries occupy these niches, entry costs for foreign businesses are high and bureaucracy is restrictive. Niches for immigrant entrepreneurship are rare, except for either within immigrant enclaves or on global markets. Results from research in Spain show that apart from enclave-related businesses, many niches in the service sector remain unoccupied by Spaniards. Allgauer (2011, p. 213) noted that "unions in Spain are less hostile towards immigration and present themselves as guardians of immigrant workers' rights," and entry costs for business and immigration remain relatively low. As a result, post-Soviet, predominantly Russian immigrants in Spain take advantage of these uncovered niches, either as individual entrepreneurs or by building innovative businesses, which in some cases led to the emergence of a Spain-based post-Soviet diaspora. Finally, Hungary has the lowest entry and immigration costs and the largest number of uncovered economic niches. In addition to limited access to the labor market, post-Soviet immigrant entrepreneurship in Hungary is the most diverse of the three analyzed countries. As Table 6.3 demonstrates, post-Soviet immigrant entrepreneurship appears in three types in Austria, five types in Spain, and six types in Hungary.

Table 6.3 Comparative classifications of post-Soviet immigrant entrepreneurship in Austria, Spain, and Hungary

Sectors and forms of post-Soviet entrepreneurship	*Type of immigrant entrepreneurship*
Austria	
Education, retail, logistics, construction, beauty self-employed, and rentals micro firms	*Grassroots* immigrant entrepreneurship
Legal, finance, media, and medical services	*Connectors* to the local market and between immigrant businesses
Real estate development, hospitality—hotels	*Corporants*/investment-based entrepreneurship
Spain	
Retail, logistics, construction, beauty self-employed, and micro firms	*Grassroots* immigrant entrepreneurship
Apartment, car, boat rentals and YouTube channels	*Individual middle-class* immigrant entrepreneurs
Additional education centers and language schools	*Connectors* of the local, Spain-based, and EU post-Soviet immigrant communities
Multisector service businesses—real estate development legal, finance, and education consulting, media, hospitality—hotels and restaurants	*Corporants*/growth-based entrepreneurship
Renewable energy, securities trade, and investment club/platform	*New exclusives* immigrant entrepreneurship
Hungary	
Food production, entertainment, real estate development and renovation micro, SME, and large companies	*Integrative* immigrant entrepreneurship
Retail, logistics, construction, retail shops, beauty services	*Grassroots* common-culture-based and transnational immigrant entrepreneurship
Media, education centers, legal and medical services	*Connectors* between the Hungarians, Hungary-based and EU post-Soviet immigrant communities
Hospitality firms—hotels and restaurants	*Corporants* immigrant entrepreneurship
IT companies	*International re-locators* immigrant entrepreneur
Multisector relatively large business	*FDI-generated* immigrant entrepreneurship

Three types of post-Soviet immigrant entrepreneurship revealed in Austria—grassroots, connectors, and corporants—were also present in Spain and Hungary, though not always within the same professions and in the same niches. For example, while post-Soviet grassroots entrepreneurs in Spain and Austria usually overlap in size and sectors, the role of connectors in Spain belongs not only to media, legal, and financial services, but also to centers of additional education. Similarly, grassroots immigrant entrepreneurship is usually small in scale and both supplied by and oriented to post-Soviet communities. Connectors are similar to grassroots immigrants in scale, supply, and market orientation, but they imply different roles within the post-Soviet immigrant communities. Both types play an important role in the legal, economic, and social integration of post-Soviet immigrants, but this integration is limited to the post-Soviet community in Austria and Hungary. In contrast, the larger geography of Spain has led to a more scattered distribution of post-Soviet communities and businesses, but digital communication has diminished and even blurred these geographical distances. These communication channels retain significance, as Kontos (2003) pointed out, in strengthening immigrant communities.

In both Austria and Hungary, major post-Soviet immigrant communities and their businesses are concentrated in Vienna and Budapest, respectively, while in Spain, they are more widespread across regions like Valencia, Andalusia, and Catalonia. The largest businesses in Austria, Spain, and Hungary, classified as corporants, operate in the real estate development, construction, and hospitality sectors. They tend to employ immigrants from former Soviet countries and serve as bridges for integration between the countries of origin of their owners and managers, the host country, and global markets. Similarly, some micro companies owned by post-Soviet immigrants with Austrian jurisdiction show potential for incremental innovation in services due to their global reach. The diversity of post-Soviet immigrant entrepreneurship in Spain also demonstrates that MME generates more diverse immigrant entrepreneurship than CME, reflected in five types of post-Soviet immigrant entrepreneurship.

The greater variety of post-Soviet entrepreneurship in Spain compared to Austria is partly due to the larger Spanish population. Despite having a similarly restrictive immigration policy as Austria due to the EU-level immigration regulations, the Spanish immigration regime is more flexible due to Spain's later modernization of its political system and economy. This creates opportunities for immigrants to take advantage of niches not yet filled by locals. Additionally, the relaxed and slow pace of Spanish operations contrasts with the more fast-paced style of post-Soviet immigrants, creating a business advantage for the latter. Therefore, post-Soviet immigrants in Spain can leverage their large communities to provide products and services that cater to their traditional needs.

The exploration of post-Soviet immigrants in Austria showed that they are highly motivated to work and start businesses due to their backgrounds in less advanced economies and poorer societies. However, they feel limited in their opportunities for growth in Austria, making entrepreneurship a crucial avenue for social mobility. In contrast, post-Soviet immigrants in Spain are driven to start businesses due to the availability of niches and low entry costs. According to Nazareno et al. (2018), the motivation for immigrant entrepreneurship depends on the pre-migration status of the immigrant. Post-Soviet newcomers in Spain are mostly limited by access to the Spanish labor market, which since Russia's invasion in Ukraine became accessible to Ukrainian citizens, while remaining equally restricted for the Russian citizens. These findings challenge generalizations about the integration of post-Soviet immigrant entrepreneurship into host country economies and suggest that factors such as the length of stay in a receiving country, as found in Finland (Johansson, 2006; Okulov, 2007), are not the only determinants. As Sanders (2022) correctly notes, the institutions that govern the allocation of financial resources vary greatly between countries and copying institutions from one country to another may not be effective.

6.5 Conclusions: The Role of Entrepreneurship in Integration of Post-Soviet Immigrants Compared across Austria, Spain, and Hungary

European countries' economic models are shaped by their post-World War II political and economic development. Similarly, immigration policies and regimes have developed as a result of these economic models, with the goal of supplying the economies with the right number and quality of workers. The demand for workers varies among economic models and over time. The role of entrepreneurship in integrating post-Soviet immigrants also varies among host countries and over time. Comparing research from Austria, Spain, and Hungary, it is evident that over half of post-Soviet immigrant entrepreneurs are women. Partially, this is due to the Soviet cultural heritage reflected through the absence of male labor force in the former Soviet Union, which led women to take on various jobs as the main breadwinners (Remennick, 2012). In post-Soviet Russia, these Soviet traditions persisted in the form of families comprising a grandmother, mother, and child, where mothers continued to play the primary role as breadwinners (Etkind, 2023).

In emigration, entrepreneurship plays a crucial role in social mobility for many post-Soviet female immigrants in Austria, Spain, and Hungary. In most cases, they view their entrepreneurial activities as an opportunity-driven process of social integration in both their new host country environment and in life-cycle changes. Therefore, in stark contrast to mainstream theories that typically depict female migrants as "overrepresented in the least desirable occupations, such as repetitive factory work, and lower-skilled positions" (Castles et al., 2019, p. 61), post-Soviet female entrepreneurs in Austria, Spain, and Hungary not only fulfill the role of main breadwinners but also serve as crucial points of contact for post-Soviet migrant communities. These women often run educational centers, Russian-language media, and theaters in Austria and Hungary. These businesses serve as contact points and communication platforms for immigrant communities and thus play a connecting role in immigrant entrepreneurship. They connect individual post-Soviet immigrants and their businesses, and, in turn, these female entrepreneurs also serve as informal leaders of post-Soviet immigrant communities at both local and national levels, extending Dunnicker and Cakir's (2016) theory of female immigrant entrepreneurship as a social mobility channel. In many cases, Russian-language media and, to a lesser extent, schools also act as communication channels between home-state institutions in host countries and the wider post-Soviet immigrant community.

Despite the close connections among post-Soviet immigrant communities in Austria, Spain, and Hungary, their lack of institutional strength and fragmentation have prevented these communities from becoming a source of political capital for their countries of origin. This fragmentation is particularly pronounced among post-Soviet immigrants in Austria, where businesses established by these immigrants do not typically have a majority of post-Soviet employees. However, primarily post-Soviet immigrant staff companies such as Alegria in Spain and 1000 Roads in Hungary work with post-Soviet-founded schools, media outlets, retail chains, and other smaller businesses and immigrant associations, meeting the needs of the immigrant community. This type of immigrant entrepreneurship highlights how immigrants, who often face challenges in their host countries and labor markets, address their socioeconomic vulnerability through serving their community (Mesch & Czamanski, 1997; Portes, 1997). This cooperation has both business and social implications, supporting the idea that social capital fosters immigrant entrepreneurship (Portes & Sensenbrenner, 1993) and distancing the immigrant community from the state structures of their countries of origin, especially concerning Russian emigrants since 2022.

Still, the bilateral relations between EU member states and the former Soviet states have shaped post-Soviet immigration to the EU to some extent. For example, the relationship between Hungary and former Soviet states like Russia and Ukraine has influenced immigration in Hungary. As Deak and Weiner (2022, p. 52) noted, "Hungary's public mood is not hostile to pro-Russian sentiments, and historical and security considerations are not the only factors on the political scene." This attitude among Hungarian political leaders, reflected in Hungary's immigration policies toward post-Soviet Russian-speaking immigrants, has created relatively favorable conditions for the development of post-Soviet entrepreneurship in Hungary. With Russia's full-scale invasion of Ukraine in February 2022, this political capital cumulated among the EU political leadership and post-Soviet political elites became even more relevant concerning the potential for integration of post-Soviet immigrant communities. In conclusion, the diversity of EU countries' economic models has led to different immigration regimes and a range of post-Soviet immigrant entrepreneurship, influencing the integration of these immigrants into their host countries.

References

Allgauer, A. (2011). Debating Integration: A Comparison of Topics and Policies in Austria and Spain. In *Looming Shadows: Migration and Integration at a Time of Upheaval* (pp. 191–219). Center for Transatlantic Relations.

Boucher, A., & Gest, J. (2018). *Crossroads: Comparative Immigration Regimes in a World of Demographic Change*. Cambridge University Press.

Castles, S., Haas, H., & Miller, M. (2019). *The Age of Migration International Population Movements in the Modern World* (6th ed.). Bloomsbury Publishing.

Deak, A., & Weiner, C. (2022). Hungary: More Business, Less Illiberalism. In *The Future of Europe and Russia: Views from the Capitals* (pp. 51–54). Springer Cham.

Dilli, S., Elert, N., & Herrmann, A. (2018). Varieties of Entrepreneurship: Exploring the Institutional Foundations of Different Entrepreneurship Types Through 'Varieties-of-Capitalism' Arguments. *Small Business Economics, 51*(2), 293–320.

Dunnecker, P., & Cakir, A. (2016). Female Migrant Entrepreneurs in Vienna: Mobility and Its Embeddedness. *Österreichische Zeitschrift für Soziologie volume, 41*, 97–113.

Etkind, A. (2023). *Russia Against Modernity* (1st ed.). Polity.

European Commission. (2021). European Website on Integration. *Governance of Migrant Integration in Hungary.*

Eurostat, 2022 Real GDP Per Capita. (2022). https://ec.europa.eu. https://ec.europa.eu/eurostat/databrowser/view/tessi190/default/table?lang=en

Hinojosa, J. (Producer). (2022, March 2). The Olive Press. *The Olive Press.* https://www.theolivepress.es/

Jessop, B. (2011). Rethinking the Diversity and Variability of Capitalism: On Variegated Capitalism in the World Market. In *Capitalist Diversity and Diversity Within Capitalism* (pp. 233–261). Routledge.

Johansson, L. (2006). *International Business Operations of Companies with Russian Involvement in Southwestern Finland.* Pan-European Institute.

Kontos, M. (2003). Self-employment Policies and Migrants' Entrepreneurship in Germany. *Entrepreneurship and Regional Development, 15*(2), 119–135.

Mesch, G., & Czamanski, D. (1997). Occupational Closure and Immigrant Entrepreneurship: Russian Jews in Israel. *The Journal of Socio-Economics, 26*(6), 597–610.

Nazareno, J., Zhou, M., & You, T. (2018). Global Dynamics of Immigrant Entrepreneurship. Changing Trends, Ethnonational Variations, and Reconceptualizations. *International Journal of Entrepreneurial Behavior & Research, 25*, 780–800.

Okulov, J. (2007). Russian Immigrant Entrepreneurship in Finland. [In Russian.]. In *In Immigrants, Multiculturalism and the World of Work* (pp. 51–80). University of Kuopio.

Portes, A. (1997). *Globalization from Below: The Rise of Transnational Communities.* Princeton University.

Portes, A., & Sensenbrenner, J. (1993). Embeddedness and Immigration: Notes on the Social Determinants of Economic Action. *American Journal of Sociology, 98*, 1320–1350.

Remennick, L. (2012). *Russian Jews on Three Continents. Identity, Integration, and Conflict.* Transaction Publisher.

Sanders, M. (2022). Enter the Prince of Denmark: Entrepreneurship for a Resilient and Sustainable Economy. *Small Business Economics, 59*, 773–779.

Sauka, A. (2008). Productive, Unproductive and Destructive Entrepreneurship: A Theoretical and Empirical Exploration.

Statistics Austria—migration. (2021–2022). https://www.statistik.at/en/statistics/population-and-society/population/migration-and-naturalisation/migration-total

Streeck, W., & Thelen, K. (2005). *Beyond Continuity: Institute of Advanced Political Economies.* Oxford University Press.

CHAPTER 7

Varieties of Post-Soviet Migrations and Entrepreneurship in the EU: Conclusions and Implications

Abstract This chapter provides an overview of the key theoretical and conceptual insights presented in this monograph and explores the practical implications of these insights, particularly concerning migration driven by the conflict in Ukraine. The chapter summarizes the major contributions of the monograph and highlights the potential real-world applications of these findings.

Keywords Post-Soviet migrations • Immigrant entrepreneurship • Economic models • Russia's invasion • Ukraine • War

7.1 Varieties of Economic Models, Immigration Regimes, and Immigrant Entrepreneurship: Major Theoretical and Conceptual Contributions

This monograph has explored the role of entrepreneurship in integrating post-Soviet immigrants in three EU countries, Austria, Spain, and Hungary. It has highlighted the connection between economic models and immigration regimes and emphasized the significance of the Varieties of Capitalism (VoC) approach in migration studies. Boucher and Gest (2018) previously recognized the relationship between countries'

S. Tepavcevic, *Diversity of Migrant Entrepreneurship in Varieties of European Capitalism*,
https://doi.org/10.1007/978-3-031-31097-3_7

economic models and immigration regimes. This monograph has furthered their work by establishing the relevance of both VoC and varieties of immigration regimes (VoIR) in studying immigration entrepreneurship. By combining comparative political economy and migration studies, this monograph provides a valuable contribution to both fields.

This monograph has explored the impact of economic models and immigration regimes on the emergence of different types of immigrant entrepreneurship, particularly among immigrants from non-EU countries, referred to as third-country nationals (TCNs). The monograph conceptualizes eight distinct types of post-Soviet immigrant entrepreneurship across Austria, Spain, and Hungary, with some types present in all three countries, while others are specific to only one or two. Table 7.1 provides an overview of all seven types found across the three countries.

The monograph differentiates between "expat" or "migrant professional" as described by Meier (2015) and "immigrant entrepreneurs" as distinct concepts. The former refers to temporary migrants driven by multinational corporations and international organizations, while the latter refers to self-motivated business persons. The analysis in Chap. 4 has shown that migrant professionals can become immigrant entrepreneurs under specific historical and geographical conditions, as seen in Hungary during the pro-democratic political and pro-market reforms in the early 1990s. In addition, the monograph has introduced a new subtype of EU immigration regime referred to as the "Extra-Union-Plus immigration regime," which is present in Hungary's DME economic model.

Table 7.1 Types of post-Soviet immigrant entrepreneurship in the three varieties of European economic models

Types of immigrant entrepreneurship	*Variety of economic model—VoC*
Grassroots immigrant entrepreneurship	CME, MME, DME
Connectors to the local market and between immigrant businesses	CME, MME, DME
Corporants/investment-based entrepreneurship	CME, MME, DME
Individual middle-class immigrant entrepreneurs	MME
New exclusives immigrant entrepreneurship	MME
Integrative immigrant entrepreneurship	DME
International re-locators immigrant entrepreneur	DME
FDI-generated immigrant entrepreneurship	DME

7.2 Theoretical Implications

The analysis in this monograph has demonstrated that the more liberal a market economy is, the more it is inclined toward the *jus soli* immigration and integration principle and the more open it is to foreign investment, the more diverse types of immigrant entrepreneurship it can generate, with a higher potential for radical innovation-driven entrepreneurship. For instance, it becomes clearer that traditional immigration countries, not only due to their LME economic model but also due to their neoliberal immigration regimes, generate the most Schumpeterian-type entrepreneurship and innovation. The findings also suggest that immigrant entrepreneurship at least in the EU is better aligned with the Austrian school of economics rather than the Schumpeterian model, supporting the argument of Vaz-Curado and Mueller (2019) that entrepreneurship is a constant individualistic-subjective approach to economic and social phenomena, simultaneously echoing Polanyi's (1944) concept of the economy's embeddedness into social processes.

Moreover, this monograph has demonstrated that immigrant entrepreneurship is rooted in the imperfections of the economies in the receiving countries and their economic and political institutional models, as well as the institutional models and imperfections in the countries of origin, particularly when considering informal social institutions. Immigrant entrepreneurship often arises at the intersections of the global economy, local mainstream economy, and the local common-culture-based migrant community economy. It is at these peripheries where these three levels of economies overlap that immigrant entrepreneurship develops. In turn, innovation is also a highly contextualized phenomenon. This leads to a significant theoretical contribution of this research, which is that immigrant entrepreneurship can be used as an indicator of globalization, and as such, comparative political economy should give greater attention to studying it. It is also important to note that economic models, even within the VoC paradigm, are approximations of a given situation at a specific point in time and suggest potential directions for future development. VoC models are dynamic and evolving and, as such, are subject to change.

7.3 Suggested Avenues for Further Research

The present monograph has highlighted the importance of further interdisciplinary research in the fields of comparative political economy, migration studies, and business studies. Additionally, potential avenue in research of immigrant entrepreneurship across other countries displaying different economic models, such as CME, MME, and DME, would deepen our understanding of migration and its impact on business and innovation. Further examination of post-Soviet and other immigrant groups in countries with different economic models, as well as comparisons between immigrant communities, would also contribute to the fields of innovation, immigrant entrepreneurship, and comparative political economy. Particularly, further exploration of entrepreneurship of Latin American and African immigrant communities in Spain, and their comparison with post-Soviet entrepreneurship would benefit scholarly literature and inform policy decisions in Spain and the EU.

Third, further research should explore the Extra-Union-Plus subtype of the EU's "Free Movement" immigration regime, found in Hungary, in other countries embodying the VoC DME economic model, such as the Czech Republic, Poland, and Slovakia. Fourth, studying immigrant entrepreneurship in post-Soviet countries can lead to significant theoretical and practical implications, if feasible given the current conflict situations. For instance, the Baltic states, being former Soviet and current EU members, have a significant Russian minority and display different economic models, ranging from LMEs to neo-corporate models. Further research on these three countries would provide a deeper understanding of post-Soviet immigrant entrepreneurship and the EU immigration regime subtypes. Additionally, non-EU post-Soviet countries like Kazakhstan, Uzbekistan, and Georgia would shed light on emigration paths, conflicts, and their sustainable resolutions. Equally important is the recognition that migrant entrepreneurship, as a social phenomenon, is profoundly gender-sensitive, particularly when examining post-Soviet immigrants in the EU. The analysis reveals that post-Soviet immigrant entrepreneurs are predominantly women, primarily because entrepreneurship offers them stable incomes. Additionally, it reinforces their position as leaders within post-Soviet migrant communities across the EU. While for post-Soviet women this societal role represents a continuation of the informal Soviet-era tradition, further research on other post-socialist female migrant groups would provide valuable insights into female migrant entrepreneurship within the European Varieties of Capitalism (VoC) framework. Overall, this monograph emphasizes the need for continued research in the areas of immigrant entrepreneurship and its role in integration and the impact of globalization on the economy and society.

7.4 Real-World Implications—Post-Soviet Migrations in the Light of the Russia-Ukraine 2022 War

Finally, as of the time of writing, Europe is facing the largest migration crisis since World War II, prompted by Russia's invasion of Ukraine. The EU has granted Ukrainians refugee status and the right to work, but the sanctions imposed by the EU on the Russian government have limited Russians' ability to immigrate to the EU. However, Spain has maintained a relatively open policy toward Russian immigration, acknowledging the humanitarian reasons for their escape from Russia.

While the ongoing conflict between the Russian army and the Ukrainian army is shaping the world order, only preliminary migration statistics are available from UNHCR (2022). According to the data, between February and December 2022, over seven million people left Ukraine, accounting for approximately 19 percent of the country's total population (UNHCR, 2022). The situation regarding emigration from Russia is even more complex, due to political and social repressions. Nevertheless, information from various sources indicates that in 2022, between three and five million people left Russia in two main waves (ERR, 2022), one from the end of February to April and another in September when the Russian government declared a "partial" mobilization (Fortune, 2022). Ukrainians primarily migrate to the EU, while Russians, facing increasingly restrictive EU visa policies, mostly flee to countries with visa-free regimes such as former Soviet countries, Georgia, Kazakhstan, Armenia, and Uzbekistan, as well as Middle Eastern countries like Turkey and the United Arab Emirates, and Serbia and Montenegro in Europe. Some of the fifteen thousand wealthiest Russians may also be among the new emigrants (The Guardian, 2022), but, as Kamalov et al. (2022) noted, it is more likely that the beneficiaries of their relocations will be Asian rather than European countries.

In the EU, post-Soviet immigrants have taken initiatives to provide aid to Ukrainian refugees. Being prevalently Russian citizens, they openly condemned Russia's government and army invasion in Ukraine, and engaged in providing relief to refugees coming from Ukraine. For instance, Ukrainian and Russian immigrants in Budapest came together to set up schools and provide accommodation for the refugees (personal communication, March 2022). Some post-Soviet-founded schools used their local administrative networks and organized accommodation for groups of refugees and even offered free education to the Ukrainian refugee children. Additionally, post-Soviet-founded companies have relocated their employees from both Ukraine and Russia. As one source noted, "We offered relocation to our colleagues from Ukraine, but most of them are bound by military duty and cannot leave the country. Nonetheless, they continue to work whenever they have access to the internet" (personal communication, November 2022). It is yet to be seen how the war in Ukraine will affect the relationships among post-Soviet immigrant communities and if it will result in the formation of separate communities based on ethnicity, as has been observed with ethnic Armenian, Georgian, Azeri, and sometimes Jewish immigrant communities and diasporas (Aron, 1991; Remennick, 2012).

Over nine months of continuous observation of discussions in various social media groups has shown that the ongoing war in Ukraine and international reactions to it are creating new division lines not only between political nations such as Russians, Ukrainians, and Belarussians, but also within these nations based on the diverse traumatic experiences of the conflict. This research suggests that successful post-Soviet immigrant businesses in the EU are likely to continue providing platforms for cooperation among representatives of countries formerly part of the Soviet Union, and that process could result in their economic and social integration in receiving countries. Additionally, the new Ukrainian, Russian, and Belarussian immigrants in the EU may group around similar experiences and cultural backgrounds, potentially leading to the formation of smaller post-CIS communities. The outcome of the war in Ukraine will also influence the formation of these groups. The excerpt from a recent emigration report illustrates the role of post-Soviet and Russian immigrant entrepreneurs in the current wave of emigration from Russia:

> This wave of Russian emigration is comprised of young, educated, and politically aware professionals who have a different vision for Russia. Their integration into earlier migrant communities is uncertain as they differ in their political views, seek new leaders, and are much younger (a generational divide in attitudes towards the war is most prominent in Russia currently). Some destinations have established Russian communities, like Central Asia, but in other places, there are no established communities. Some have taken a post-colonial approach, interacting with locals in their local language, even in complex languages like Armenian or Georgian. The main challenge for these emigres is feeling lost and disoriented, with little support from their

sending communities, and fear of discrimination and lack of opportunities in receiving societies. Self-organization and support from various entrepreneurs is what keeps them afloat. (Kamalov et al., 2022)

To address the migration crisis, the following three suggestions are offered instead of an epilogue. First, a nuanced approach is necessary to prevent the violation of human rights for Russian and Belarussian emigrants and refugees, which is widely practiced by the current Russian authorities. Second, the EU should have closer engagement with countries with authoritarian regimes to prevent violent conflicts and migration crises. Finally yet importantly, improved multilevel coordination within the EU will also help prevent violent conflicts and migration crises within the continent.

References

Aron, L. (1991). *Preparing America for the Wave of Russian Immigrants.* Heritage Foundation.

Boucher, A., & Gest, J. (2018). *Crossroads: Comparative Immigration Regimes in a World of Demographic Change.* Cambridge University Press.

ERR. (2022, August 25). S nachala voiny rossijane vhezzhayut v evrosojuz v osnovom cherez finljaniju i estoniju.

Fortune. (2022, October 18). Russia's Population Is in a Historic Decline as Emigration, War and a Plunging Birth Rate Form a 'perfect storm'. https://fortune.com/2022/10/18/russia-population-historic-decline-emigration-war-plunging-birth-rate-form-perfect-storm/

Kamalov, E., Kostenko, V., Sergeeva, I., & Zavadskaya, M. (2022). *Russia's 2022 Anti-War Exodus: The Attitudes and Expectations of Russian Migrants.*

Meier, L. (2015). *Migrant Professionals in the City. Local Encounters, Identities and Inequalities.* Routledge.

Polanyi, K. (1944). *The Great Transformation: The Political and Economic Origins of Our Time.* Beacon Press.

Remennick, L. (2012). *Russian Jews on Three Continents. Identity, Integration, and Conflict.* Transaction Publisher.

The Guardian. (2022, June 13). More Than 15,000 Millionaires Expected to Leave Russia in 2022.

UNHCR. (2022). Operational Data Portal – Ukraine Refugee Situation.

Vaz-Curado, F., & Mueller, A. (2019). The Concept of Entrepreneur of Schumpeter in Comparison to Kirzner. *Interdisciplinary Journal of Philosophy Law and Economics, 7*(3), 613–642.

Bibliography

. (2016). *Russkaja Gostinaja*. https://www.russkajagostinaja.at

. (2022). *Luxury Immibilien*. https://luxury-vienna.com/about-us

Acs, Z., Auito, E., & Szerb, L. (2014). *Global Entrepreneurship and Development Index 2014*.

Adams, T., Ellis, C., & S., H.-J. (2017). Autoethnography. In *The International Encyclopedia of Communication Research Methods*. John Wiley & Sons, Inc.

Aldrich, H., & Zimmer, C. (1986). Entrepreneurship Through Social Networks. In *The Art and Science of Entrepreneurship* (pp. 3–23). Ballinger Publishing Company.

Alegria. (2010–2023).

Allgauer, A. (2011). Debating Integration: A Comparison of Topics and Policies in Austria and Spain. In *Looming Shadows: Migration and Integration at a Time of Upheaval* (pp. 191–219). Center for Transatlantic Relations.

Anderson, B. (1991). *Imagined Communities: Reflections on the Origin and Spread of Nationalism*. Verso.

Anderson, S., & Platzer, M. (2006). *American Made: The Impact of Immigrant Entrepreneurs and Professionals on U.S. Competitiveness*. National Venture Capital Association.

Aron, L. (1991). *Preparing America for the Wave of Russian Immigrants*. Heritage Foundation.

Artyunov, A. A. (2017). Spanish Immigrants and the Institute of Citizenship in the USSR (The Second Half of 1930s and the Beginning of 1940s). *RUDN Journal of World History, 9*(2), 132–138.

S. Tepavcevic, *Diversity of Migrant Entrepreneurship in Varieties of European Capitalism*,
https://doi.org/10.1007/978-3-031-31097-3

Aslund, A. (2007). *How Capitalism was Built. The Transformation of Central and Eastern Europe, Russia and Central Asia*. Cambridge University Press.

Audretsch, D., Bönte, W., & Tamvada, J. (2013). Religion, Social Class, and Entrepreneurial Choice. *Journal of Business Venturing, 28*(6), 774–789.

Austria Government (Producer). (2019, January 1). Federal Government's Official Information Website on Migration to Austria. *www.migration.gv.at*. https://www.migration.gv.at/en/living-and-working-in-austria/integration-and-citizenship/integration-agreement/

Ballester, R., Velazco, J., & Rigall-I-Torrent, R. (2015). Effects of the Great Recession on Immigrants' Household Consumption in Spain. *Social Indicators Research, 123*(3), 771–797.

Barcelona.ru. (2020). https://barcelona.ru/

Baubock, R. (2006). *Migration and Citizenship. Legal Status, Rights and Political Participation*. Amsterdam University Press.

Baumol, W. (1993). Formal Entrepreneurship Theory in Economics: Existence and Bounds. *Journal of Business Venturing, 8*(3), 197–210.

Baycan, T., & Nijkamp, P. (2006). *Migrant Female Entrepreneurship – Driving Forces, Motivation and Performance* (2006–18).

Baycan, T., & Nijkamp, P. (2007). *Migrant Entrepreneurship in a Diverse Europe: In Search of Sustainable Development.*

Bikova, E. (2011). Baturina pokupaet centr Vienny. *Euromag*. https://www.euromag.ru/economics/baturina-pokupaet-centr-veny/

Biro-Nagy, A. (2021). Orbán's Political Jackpot: Migration and the Hungarian Electorate. *Journal of Ethnic and Migration Studies, 48*(2), 405–424.

Boettke, P., & Coyne, C. (2009). *Context Matters: Institutions and Entrepreneurship*. https://doi.org/10.1561/0300000018

Bohle, D., & Greskovits, B. (2012). *Capitalist Diversity on Europe's Periphery*. Cornell University Press.

Bosma, N., Concent, J., Sanders, M. W., & Stam, E. (2018). Institutions, Entrepreneurship, and Economic Growth in Europe. *Small Business Economics, 51*(4).

Boucher, A., & Gest, J. (2018). *Crossroads: Comparative Immigration Regimes in a World of Demographic Change*. Cambridge University Press.

Brubacker, R. (1992). *Citizenship and Nationhood in France and Germany*. Harvard University Press.

Bruquetas Cellejo, M., Garces-Mascarenas, B., Moren-Alegret, R., Penninx, R., & Ruiz-Vieytez, E. (2011). The Case of Spain. In *Migration Policymaking in Europe: The Dynamics of Actors and Contexts in Past and Present* (pp. 291–323). Amsterdam University Press.

Bruquetas-Callejo, M., & Perna, R. (2020). Migration and Healthcare Reforms in Spain: Symbolic Politics, Converging Outputs, Oppositions from the Field. *South European Society and Politics, 25*(1), 75–98.

Brzozowski, J., & Pedziwiatr, K. (2016). *Pushed to the Mainstream Market: The Case of Immigrant Entrepreneurs in Lesser Poland*. Paper Presented at the Cross-Border Migration and its Implications for the Central European Area, Bratislava.

Byford, A. (2012). The Russian Diaspora in International Relations: "Compatriots" in Britain. *Europe-Asia Studies, 64*(4), 715–735.

Caliandro, A. (2014). *The Difference Between Netnography and Digital Ethnography*.

Castles, S. (1995). How Nation-States Respond to Immigration and Ethnic Diversity. *Journal of Ethnic and Migration Studies, 21*(3), 293–308.

Castles, S., Haas, H., & Miller, M. (2019). *The Age of Migration International Population Movements in the Modern World* (6th ed.). Bloomsbury Publishing.

Chervona Kalyna. (n.d.).

Cole, G. D. H., & Postgate, R. (1946). *The Common People 1746–1946*. Methuen.

Commission, E. (2022). EU Sanctions Against Russia Following the Invasion of Ukraine. https://eu-solidarity-ukraine.ec.europa.eu/eu-sanctions-against-russia-following-invasion-ukraine_en

Csaba, L. (2007). *The New Political Economy of Emerging Europe*. Akademiai Kiado.

Deak, A., & Weiner, C. (2022). Hungary: More Business, Less Illiberalism. In *The Future of Europe and Russia: Views from the Capitals* (pp. 51–54). Springer Cham.

Dilli, S., Elert, N., & Herrmann, A. (2018). Varieties of Entrepreneurship: Exploring the Institutional Foundations of Different Entrepreneurship Types Through 'Varieties-of-Capitalism' Arguments. *Small Business Economics, 51*(2), 293–320.

Drahokuopil, J., & Myant, M. (2016). Dependent Capitalism and Employment Relations in East Central Europe. In *Social Transformations in Central and Eastern Europe: Europeanization and Beyond* (pp. 42–59). Routledge.

Drucker, P. F. (1986). *Innovation and Entrepreneurship: Practice and Principles*. Harper & Row.

Dunnecker, P., & Cakir, A. (2016). Female Migrant Entrepreneurs in Vienna: Mobility and Its Embeddedness. *Österreichische Zeitschrift für Soziologie, 41*, 97–113.

Ebner, A. (2015). Editorial: Exploring Regional Varieties of Capitalism. *Regional Studies, 50*(1), 3–6.

Economic Policy Reforms. (2014).

ERR. (2022, August 25). S nachala voiny rossijane vhezzhayut v evrosojuz v osnovom cherez finljaniju i estoniju.

Ershov, V. F., & Gadzieva, K. K. (2018). Russian Community in Spain and Cultural Dialogue (1991–2015). *RUDN Journal of Russian History, 17*(1), 92–108.

Espana Rusa. (2020). *Espanarusa*. https://espanarusa.com/

Etkind, A. (2023). *Russia Against Modernity* (1st ed.). Polity.

European Commission. (2021). European Website on Integration. *Governance of migrant integration in Hungary.*

European Commission, M. a. H. A. (2023). Migration Management: Welcoming Refugees from Ukraine. https://home-affairs.ec.europa.eu/policies/migration-and-asylum/migration-management/migration-management-welcoming-refugees-ukraine_en

European Parliament. (2016). Regulation (EU) 2016/399 of the European Parliament and of the Council of 9 March 2016 on a Union Code on the Rules Governing the Movement of Persons Across Borders (Schengen Borders Code).

Eurostat (2021). https://ec.europa.eu/eurostat/statistics-explained/index.php?title=Migration_and_migrant_population_statistics

Eurostat, 2022 Real GDP Per Capita. (2022). https://ec.europa.eu. https://ec.europa.eu/eurostat/databrowser/view/tessi190/default/table?lang=en

Feldmann, M. (2019). Global Varieties of Capitalism. *World Politics, 71*(1), 162–196.

Fortune. (2022, October 18). Russia's Population Is in a Historic Decline as Emigration, War and a Plunging Birth Rate Form a 'perfect storm'. https://fortune.com/2022/10/18/russia-population-historic-decline-emigration-war-plunging-birth-rate-form-perfect-storm/

FreeDa Language Space. (2017). https://freedaspace.com/en/

Galletti, F. (2018). Institutions of Coordination in Mixed Market Economies: The Gatekeeper Role of the State in Labour Relations. *Sociology and Anthropology, 6*(7), 589–601.

Global Entrepreneurship Monitor (Producer). (2021). Entrepreneurial Behaviour and Attitudes, Austria. https://www.gemconsortium.org/economy-profiles/austria-2

González-Ferrer, A., & Moreno-Fuentes, F. J. (2017). Back to the Suitcase? Emigration During the Great Recession in Spain. *South European Society and Politics, 22*(4), 447–471.

Graham, L. (2013). *Lonely Ideas. Can Russia Compete?* The MIT Press.

Gustafson, T. (1999). *Capitalism – Russian Style.* Cambridge University Press.

Hall, P. A., & Soskice, D. (2001). *Varieties of Capitalism: The Institutional Foundations of Comparative Advantage.* Oxford University Press.

Halse, L. (2022). What's an Immigration Regime? Exploring Migration Patterns Worldwide.

Hancké, B. (2009). *Debating Varieties of Capitalism: A Reader.* Oxford University Press.

Hancké, B., Rhodes, M., & Thatcher, M. (2007). *Beyond Varieties of Capitalism: Conflict, Contradiction, and Complementarities in the European Economy.* Oxford University Press.

Heleniak, T. (2017). Post-Soviet Russian-Speaking Migration to the UK: The Discourses of Visibility and Accountability. In *Post-soviet Migration and Diasporas: From Global Perspectives to Everyday Practices.* Palgrave Pivot.

Henrekson, M., & Rosenberg, N. (2000). Designing Efficient Institutions for Science-Based Entrepreneurship: Lesson from the US and Sweden. *Journal of Technology Transfer, 26*(3), 207–231.

Herrmann, A. (2019). A Plea for Varieties of Entrepreneurship. *Small Business Economics, 52*(2), 331–343.

Herrmann, A. (2020). On the Institutional Foundations of the Varieties of Entrepreneurship in Europe. In *The Entrepreneurial Society. International Studies in Entrepreneurship* (Vol. 44, pp. 331–343). Springer.

Hinojosa, J. (Producer). (2022, March 2). The Olive Press. *The Olive Press.* https://www.theolivepress.es/

Honositas eddig 230 ezer allampolgarsagi kerelem erkezett. (2012, March 14).

Huddleston, T., Niessen, J., Ni Chaoimh, E., & White, E. (2011). *Migrant Integration Policy Index II.* British Council and Migration Policy Group.

Hughes, J. (1983). Arthur Cole and Entrepreneurial History. *Business and Economic History, 12.*

Hungary IOM. (2022). https://hungary.iom.int/

International Migration Outlook 2012. (2012).

IOM Report 2018. (2018).

IOM Report 2020. (2020).

Jessop, B. (2011). Rethinking the Diversity and Variability of Capitalism: On Variegated Capitalism in the World Market. In *Capitalist Diversity and Diversity Within Capitalism* (pp. 233–261). Routledge.

Johansson, L. (2006). *International Business Operations of Companies with Russian Involvement in Southwestern Finland.*

Kamalov, E., Kostenko, V., Sergeeva, I., & Zavadskaya, M. (2022). *Russia's 2022 Anti-War Exodus: The Attitudes and Expectations of Russian Migrants.*

Khanenko-Friesen, N. (2017). Migrant Self-Reflectivity and New Ukrainian Diaspora in Southern Europe: The Case of Portugal. In *Post-Soviet Migration and Diasporas. From Global Perspectives to Everyday Practices* (pp. 47–63). Springer International Publishing.

King, L. P. (2007). Central European Capitalism in Comparative Perspective. In *Beyond Varieties of Capitalism: Conflict, Contradiction and Complementarities in the European Economy* (pp. 307–327). Oxford University Press.

Kontos, M. (2003). Self-employment Policies and Migrants' Entrepreneurship in Germany. *Entrepreneurship and Regional Development, 15*(2), 119–135.

Kovacevic-Bielicki, D., & Pejovic, A. (2020). *Extreme Digital Push in a World Changed by COVID-19: Experiences and Reflections on Doing Social Research Online.*

Kozinets, R. (2015). *Netnography. Doing Ethnographic Research Online.* SAGE.

Kraler, A. (2011). The Case of Austria. In *Migration Policymaking in Europe. The Dynamics of Actors and Contexts in Past and Present*. Amsterdam University Press, IMSCOE.

Kshetri, N. (2009). Entrepreneurship in Post-Socialist Economies: A Typology and Institutional Contexts for Market Entrepreneurship. *Journal of International Entrepreneurship, 7*(3), 236–259.

Kuznetsov, A. (2007). *The internationalization of the Russian economy: Innovative aspect (In Russian)*. URSS.

Kuznetsov, A. (2011). *Outward FDI from Russia and its Policy Context.*

Leadem, R. (2017). The Immigrant Entrepreneurs Behind Major American Companies. *www.entrepreneur.com*. https://www.entrepreneur.com/article/288687

Lee, E. S. (1966). A Theory of Migration. *Demography, 3*(1), 47–57.

Light, I. (1984). Immigrant and Ethnic Enterprise in North America. *Ethnic and Racial Studies, 7*(2), 195–216.

Liuhto, K. (2005). *Expansion or Exodus: Why Do Russian Corporations Invest Abroad?* Routledge.

Marchand, K., & Siegel, M. (2015). *World Migration Report 2015: Immigrant Entrepreneurship in Cities – Background Paper.*

Matricano, D., & Sorenttino, M. (2014). Ukrainian Entrepreneurs in Italy: Factors Influencing the Creation of Ethnic Ventures. *Journal of Innovation and Entrepreneurship, 3*(10).

Meier, L. (2015). *Migrant Professionals in the City. Local Encounters, Identities and Inequalities.* Routledge.

Mesch, G., & Czamanski, D. (1997). Occupational Closure and Immigrant Entrepreneurship: Russian Jews in Israel. *The Journal of Socio-Economics, 26*(6), 597–610.

Migrants Refugees – Country Profile Spain. (2020).

Milgrom, P., North, D., & Weingast, B. (1990). The Role of Institutions in the Revival of Trade: The Law Merchant, Private Judges, and the Champagne Fairs. *Economics and Politics, 2*(1), 1–23.

Miller, D. (2018). *Digital Anthropology. Cambridge Encyclopedia of Anthropology.*

Molina, O., & Rhodes, M. (2007). The Political Economy of Adjustment in Mixed Market Economies: A Study of Spain and Italy. In *Beyond Varieties of Capitalism* (pp. 223–252). Oxford University Press.

Molodikova, I. (2014). Russian Policy Toward Compatriots: Diversities and Contradictions of Its Implementation. In *Post-Soviet Diasporas: Identities, Linkages, and Transformation* (pp. 20–21).

Molodikova, I. (2019). Muslim Refugees from Russia: Do the Chechens Bring Their Own "aul" from Chechnya to the EU? In *In Muslim Minorities and the Refugee Crisis in Europe. Narratives and Policy Responses* (p. 339). SGH.

Moricz, I. (Producer). (2013). An Overview of the Migration Policies and Trends – Hungary. https://migrationonline.cz

Munkejord, M. C. (2017). Local and Transnational Networking Among Female Immigrant Entrepreneurs in Peripheral Rural Contexts: Russian Female Entrepreneurs in Norway. *European Urban and Regional Studies, 24*(1), 7–20.

Myant, M., & Drahokoupil, J. (2011). *Transition Economies: Political Economy in Russia, Eastern Europe, and Central Asia*. John Wiley and Sons, Inc.

Mykhenko, V. (2007). Strengths and Weaknesses of 'Weak' Coordination: Economic Institutions, Revealed Comparative Advantages, and Socio-Economic Performance of Mixed Market Economies in Poland and Ukraine. In *Beyond Varieties of Capitalism: Conflict, Contradictions, and Complementarities in the European Economy* (pp. Chapter 13). Oxford University Press.

Nagy, B., Ligeti, M., & Martin, J. P. (2016). *In Whose Interest?: Shadows Over the Hungarian Residency Bond Program*. Investment Migration Council.

Nazareno, J., Zhou, M., & You, T. (2018). Global Dynamics of Immigrant Entrepreneurship. Changing Trends, Ethnonational Variations, and Reconceptualizations. *International Journal of Entrepreneurial Behavior & Research, 25*, 780–800.

New Viennese Journal. (2020, May). https://nwm.at/nvz/archive

Nölke, A., & Vliegenthart, A. (2009). Enlarging the Varieties of Capitalism: The Emergence of Dependent Market Economies in East Central Europe. *World Politics, 61*(4), 670–702.

North, D. C. (1991). Institutions. *The Journal of Economic Perspectives, 5*(1), 97–112.

Okulov, J. (2007). Russian Immigrant Entrepreneurship in Finland. [In Russian.]. In *In Immigrants, Multiculturalism and the World of Work* (pp. 51–80). University of Kuopio.

Orban, A. (2008). *Power, Energy, and the New Russian Imperialism*. Praeger Security International.

Orozco, M. (2008). *Tasting Identity: Trends in Migrant Demand for Home-Country Goods.*

Pavlinek, P. (2016). Whose Success? The State-Foreign Capital Nexus and the Development of the. *European Urban and Regional Studies, 23*(4), 571–593.

Pejovich, S. (1999). The Effects of the Interaction of Formal and Informal Institutions on Social Stability and Economic Development. *Journal of Markets and Morality, 2*(2), 164–181.

Perchinig, B. (2013). *10 Observations on the Future of Migration: Costs, Benefits and Policy Responses.*

Pink, S., Horst, H., Postill, J., Hjorth, L., Lewis, T., & Tacchi, J. (2016). *Digital Ethnography: Principles and Practice*. Sage Publications.

Platt, L., Polavieja, J., & J., R. (2021). Which Integration Policies Work? The Heterogeneous Impact of National Institutions on Immigrants' Labor Market Attainment in Europe. *International Migration Review, 56*, 344–375.

Polanyi, K. (1944). *The Great Transformation: The Political and Economic Origins of Our Time*. Beacon Press.
Portes, A. (1997). *Globalization from Below: The Rise of Transnational Communities*. Princeton University.
Portes, A., & Sensenbrenner, J. (1993). Embeddedness and Immigration: Notes on the Social Determinants of Economic Action. *American Journal of Sociology, 98*, 1320–1350.
Portes, A., Wilson, W., & K. L. (1980). Immigrant Enclaves An Analysis of the Labor Market Experiences of Cubans in Miami. *The American Journal of Sociology, 86*, 295–319.
"Pravda" Program. (2016, October 24).
Rabota dlya nelegala. (2021).
Rath, J. (2006). *Entrepreneurship Among Migrants and Returnees: Creating New Opportunities*, Turin.
Reax. (1997–2022). https://reax.hu/
Remennick, L. (2012). *Russian Jews on Three Continents. Identity, Integration, and Conflict*. Transaction Publisher.
Ren, N., & Liu, H. (2015). Traversing Between Transnationalism and Integration: Dual Embeddedness of New Chinese Immigrant Entrepreneurs in Singapore. *Asian and Pacific Migration Journal, 24*(3), 298–326.
Research Summaries. (2022).
Rodgers, P., Vershanina, N., Williams, C., & Theodorakopoulos, N. (2018). Leveraging Symbolic Capital: The Use of Blat Networks Across Transnational Spaces. *Global Networks, 19*(1), 119–136.
Royo, S. (2014). Institutional Degeneration and the Economic Crisis in Spain. *American Behavioral Scientist, 58*(12), 1568–1591.
. RussianInn. (2019, October).
Ryazantsev, S. (2015). The Modern Russian-Speaking Communities in the World: Formation, Assimilation and Adaptation in Host Societies. *Mediterranean Journal of Social Sciences, 6*(3S4).
Ryazantsev, S. (2017). "Russian-Russian" Economy as Mechanism of the Integration of Russian-Speaking Migrants in the Receiving Countries. *Journal of Economic, 25*(1).
Ryazantsev, S., Pismennaya, E., Lukyantsev, A., Sivoplyasova, S., & Khramova, M. (2018). Modern Emigration from Russia and Formation of Russian-Speaking Communities Abroad (In Russian). *World Economy and International Relations, 62*(6), 93–107.
Sahin, M., Nijkamp, P., & Baycan-Levent, T. (2006). Migrant Entrepreneurship from the Perspective of Cultural Diversity. *Series Research Memoranda, 16*.
Sahin, M., Nijkamp, P., & Suzuki, S. (2013). Survival of the Fittest Among Migrant Entrepreneurs. In *A Study on Differences in the Efficiency Performance*

of Migrant Entrepreneurs in Amsterdam by Means of Data Envelopment Analysis. Faculty of Economics and Business Administration.

Sanders, M. (2022). Enter the Prince of Denmark: Entrepreneurship for a Resilient and Sustainable Economy. *Small Business Economics, 59*, 773–779.

Sassen, S. (1991). *The Global City.* Princeton University Press.

Sauka, A. (2008). Productive, Unproductive and Destructive Entrepreneurship: A Theoretical and Empirical Exploration.

Schneider, B. R. (2013). *Hierarchical Capitalism in Latin America: Business, Labor, and the Challenges of Equitable Development.* Cambridge University Press.

Schumpeter, J. (1934). *The Theory of Economic Development.* Harvard University Press.

Scott, W. R. (2008). Approaching Adulthood: The Maturing of Institutional Theory. *Theory and Society. Special Issue on Theorizing Institutions: Current Approaches and Debates, 37*(5), 427–442.

Shvarts, A. (2010). Elite Entrepreneurs from the Former Soviet Union: How They Made Their Millions. PhD Dissertation.

Skageby, J. (2011). Online Ethnographic Methods: Towards a Qualitative Understanding of Virtual Community Practices. In *Handbook of Research on Methods and Techniques for Studying Virtual Communities: Paradigms and Phenomena* (pp. 410–428). IGI Global.

Statistics Austria—Migration. (2021–2022). https://www.statistik.at/en/statistics/population-and-society/population/migration-and-naturalisation/migration-total

Streeck, W., & Thelen, K. (2005). *Beyond Continuity: Institute of Advanced Political Economies.* Oxford University Press.

Su, J., Zhai, Q., & Karlsson, T. (2017). Beyond Red Tape and Fools: Institutional Theory in Entrepreneurship Research, 1992–2014. *Entrepreneurship Theory and Practice, 41*(4), 505–531.

Szczepanikova, A. (2008). Settlement and (re) construction of Gender Relations in Exile: Chechen Refugees in Eastern Europe in Chechens in the European Union. In A. Janda, N. Leitner, & M. Vogl (Eds.), *Chechens in the European Union.* Österreichischer Integrationfonds (Federal Ministry of Interior).

Tepavcevic, S. (2013). Russian Foreign Policy and Outward Foreign Direct Investments: Cooperation, Subordination, Or Disengagement? Ph.D. Dissertation.

Tepavcevic, S. (2017). Immigrant Entrepreneurship in the Post-Socialist Countries of the European Union: Motives and Patterns of Entrepreneurship of Post-Soviet Immigrants in Hungary. *Migration and Ethnic Themes, 1*, 65–92.

Tepavcevic, S. (2018). In the Bear's Shadow? Russia's International Image and Its Influence on Investments of Russian Companies in Post-Socialist Europe. *Journal of East-West Business, 24*(2), 108–137.

Tepavcevic, S. (2020a). *Homo Sovieticus Or the Agent of Change?*

Tepavcevic, S. (2021). Changing Geography, Retaining the Mentality: Social and Economic Integration of Post-Soviet Immigrants in Austria and Hungary. *Review of Economic Theory and Policy, 3*, 137–154.

Tepavcevic, S., Molodikova, I., & Ryazantsev, S. (2020). Post-Soviet Russian-Language Migration, Investment, and Entrepreneurship in Eastern and Central Europe (for Example of Hungary, Austria, and the Czech Republic). *Today and Tomorrow of the Russian Economy [In Russian], 99–100*, 5–22.

The Guardian. (2022, June 13). More Than 15,000 Millionaires Expected to Leave Russia in 2022.

Thornton, P., Lounsbury, M., & Ocasio, W. (2012). *The Institutional Logics Perspective: A New Approach to Culture, Structure, and Process*. Oxford University Press.

Tirpitz, A., Groll, C., & Ghane, K. (2011). *Russian Companies Enter Germany*.

Turaeva, R. (2022). Measuring Humans Through Money: Anthropology of Debt in Post-Soviet Economies. *Social Lives of Debts: Ethnographies from Post-Soviet and Post-socialist Economies, 1*(6).

TVRain. (2019, October). Hard Days Night.

UNHCR. (2022). Operational Data Portal – Ukraine Refugee Situation.

Union, C. o. t. E. (2023). Infographic – Refugees from Ukraine in the EU. https://www.consilium.europa.eu/en/infographics/ukraine-refugees-eu/

Van Mol, C., & de Valk, H. (2016). Migration and Immigrants in Europe: A Historical and Demographic Perspective. In *Integration Processes and Policies in Europe* (pp. 31–55). Springer.

Vaz-Curado, F., & Mueller, A. (2019). The Concept of Entrepreneur of Schumpeter in Comparison to Kirzner. *Interdisciplinary Journal of Philosophy Law and Economics, 7*(3), 613–642.

Waldinger, R. (2009). Beyond Transnationalism: An Alternative Perspective on Immigrants' Homeland Connections. In *Oxford Handbook of the Politics of International Relations* (pp. 74–102). Oxford University Press.

Walter, A., & Zhang, X. (2012). *East Asian Capitalism: Diversity, Continuity, and Change*. Oxford University Press.

Weinar, A. (2018). Politics of Emigration in Europe. In *The Routledge Handbook of the Politics of Migration in Europe* (pp. 62–73). Routledge.

Weiner, C. (2015). Tracking Russian FDI in Hungary. *East European Studies, 6*, 120–168. http://real.mtak.hu/34126/1/Weiner_Tracking....pdf

Wesch, M. (2009). YouTube and You: Experiences of Self-awareness in the Context Collapse of the Recording Webcam. *Explorations in Media Ecology, 8*(2), 19–34.

Whitley, R. (2003). Changing Transnational Institutions and Management of International Business. In *Globalization and Institutions* (pp. 108–133). Edward Elgar.

World Bank National Accounts Data, Austria GDP Growth. (2022). www.worldbank.org. https://data.worldbank.org/indicator/NY.GDP.MKTP.KD.ZG?locations=AT

Zavadskaya, M. (2022). Anti-war Wave of Emigration: Should I Stay Or Should I Go? Retrieved from Riddle website: https://ridl.io/anti-war-wave-of-nbsp-emigration-should-i-nbsp-stay-or-nbsp-should-i-nbsp-go/

Zhou, M. (2004). Revising Ethnic Entrepreneurship: Convergencies, Controversies, and Conceptual Advancements. *International Migration Review, 38*(3), 1040–1074.

Zimmerman, K. F. (2005). *European Migration. What Do We Know?* Oxford University Press.

Index

S. Tepavcevic, *Diversity of Migrant Entrepreneurship in Varieties of European Capitalism*,
https://doi.org/10.1007/978-3-031-31097-3

The manufacturer's authorised representative in the EU is Springer Nature Customer Service Centre GmbH, Europaplatz 3, 69115 Heidelberg, Germany. If you have any concerns regarding our products, please contact ProductSafety@springernature.com

Printed and bound by CPI Group (UK) Ltd, Croydon, CR0 4YY
28/09/2026
02224072-0019